# Private Investigation and Homeland Security

# Private Investigation and Homeland Security

**Daniel J. Benny, PhD**

CRC Press
Taylor & Francis Group
Boca Raton London New York

CRC Press is an imprint of the
Taylor & Francis Group, an **informa** business

CRC Press
Taylor & Francis Group
6000 Broken Sound Parkway NW, Suite 300
Boca Raton, FL 33487-2742

First issued in paperback 2021

ISBN-13: 978-0-367-77917-7 (pbk)
ISBN-13: 978-1-4987-7397-3 (hbk)

---

### Library of Congress Cataloging-in-Publication Data

---

Names: Benny, Daniel J., author.
Title: Private investigation and homeland security / by Dr. Daniel J. Benny.
Description: Boca Raton, FL : CRC Press, [2017] | Includes bibliographical references and
  index.
Identifiers: LCCN 2016026645| ISBN 9781498773973 (hardback : alk. paper) | ISBN
  9781315317243 (ebook)
Subjects: LCSH: Private investigators--United States. | Private security services--United
  States. | National security--United States. | Internal security--United States.
Classification: LCC HV8088 .B46 2017 | DDC 363.32--dc23
LC record available at https://lccn.loc.gov/2016026645

---

**Visit the Taylor & Francis Web site at**
**http://www.taylorandfrancis.com**

**and the CRC Press Web site at**
**http://www.crcpress.com**

This book is dedicated to my daughter Allison, her husband Kurt Cranford, and my five grandchildren: Phaydra Cranford, Carter Cranford, Keira Cranford, Amelia Cranford, and Lennon Cranford.

# Contents

# Preface

The threat against the homeland continues, and the private investigator plays a critical part in this effort. This includes providing criminal, civil, and background investigations; protective service; security consulting; and electronic sweeps. This book will provide an overview of the role of private investigation in protection of the homeland, and will show how such skills can be utilized by businesses and governments in this effort.

I would like to thank the United Network Command for Law and Enforcement, without whose assistance this book would not have been possible.

I also thank Sherlock Holmes, the Association of British Investigators, the World Association of Detectives, and Sandi Davies with the International Foundation for Protection Officers.

# Author

 **Daniel J. Benny, PhD**, is a licensed private investigator and security consultant working from Harrisburg, Pennsylvania. He earned his PhD in criminal justice from Capella University and is a graduate of the U.S. Naval War College. He holds many certifications in security, including a Certified Protection Professional (CPP) and Professional Certified Investigator (PCI) with ASIS International; a Certified Fraud Examiner (CFE) with the Association of Certified Fraud Examiners; and a Certified Confidentiality Officer (CCO) by the Business Espionage Controls and Countermeasures Association. He has served as a U.S. Navy Intelligence officer with an assignment with the Office of Naval Intelligence, Naval Investigative Service (NIS) and the Central Intelligence Agency (CIA) as well as a Navy police chief. He is a member of many organizations on security and has authored several books on the subject published by CRC Press.

# Chapter 1

# Historical Overview of Private Investigation

## Myths and the Private Investigator

The image that many have of the private investigator is based primarily upon myths and legends portrayed in novels and films, and on television. Some of these images portray the private investigator as a bigger-than-life hero, while others show the investigator as a seedy, unethical character who will do anything for money. Both of these unrealistic perceptions can have an enormous impact on the image of the real private investigator.

The myths of the private investigator began in the spring of 1886 with the introduction of Sherlock Holmes in the publication *A Study in Scarlet*, by Sir Arthur Conan Doyle. This character was so well received that Doyle went on to write 3 additional full-length novels and 56 short stories. The appeal of the Sherlock Holmes character continues today, not only through the reprinting of the books and stories, but also in film, television, and play productions.

The image portrayed by the character of Sherlock Holmes is a positive one. Holmes is an intelligent, honest, and professional investigator, but his independent nature often puts him at odds with the police. This independence established a basic characteristic for the fictional private investigator, which can be observed in characters such as Raymond Chandler's Philip Marlowe and Dashiell Hammett's Sam Spade, as portrayed by Humphrey Bogart in the 1941 Warner Brothers film *The Maltese Falcon*.

With the advent of television, an entire new arena was opened for the fictional private investigator. Television, more than any other medium, has influenced how people perceive the private investigator. Since the early days of television, not a season has gone by without a private investigator series, beginning with *Richard Diamond* and *77 Sunset Strip* in the late 1950s and continuing with *Mannix* and *Honey West* in the 1960s; *Harry O* and *The Rockford Files* in the 1970s; and *Magnum, P.I.* and *The Equalizer* in later years. The overall impression given by television private investigators is that of a likeable individual trying to do the best possible job for the client, but occasionally resorting to unethical and at times illegal methods to achieve their goals. This of course is not the reality of private investigators who work for their clients in protecting their interests and preserving homeland security.

## Sherlock Holmes and Homeland Security

The role of the private investigator and homeland security can be traced back to Sherlock Holmes (Figure 1.1). While most of the cases of Holmes involved working for individual clients on both civil and criminal matters, Holmes also worked for the Crown and the British government on cases of national security, and what is now called homeland security. This included the case of *The Naval Treaty* and *The Adventure of the Bruce-Partington Plans*.

In *The Naval Treaty*, a vital document related to England and a naval treaty are stolen from a clerk in the British Foreign Office. Disclosure of the document

**Figure 1.1    Sherlock Holmes, consulting detective. (Photograph by Daniel J. Benny.)**

would have a serious negative impact on the British government. Holmes is asked to investigate the theft and recover the document, which he does. Holmes conducts an investigation related to homeland security in *The Adventure of the Bruce-Partington Plans*. In this matter, Holmes investigates the death of a government clerk from the British Royal Arsenal and the theft of the plans for the *Bruce-Partington Submarine*. The death of the clerk and the missing submarine plans are a threat to the British homeland. In the end, Holmes solves the murder and recovers the *Bruce-Partington Submarine* plans.

While Holmes's cases are fictional, they do demonstrate how a private investigator could perform an investigation in support of homeland security. In fact, when a private investigator begins an investigation, one never knows where it might lead or how it may be of singular importance to the protection of the homeland.

## Allan Pinkerton and Homeland Security

The development of private investigation as a profession began in a similar time period as its fictional counterpart Sherlock Holmes. Although private investigators had been offering services in the early 1800s, it was not until 1850, with the formation of the Pinkerton Detective Agency, that the first professional and organized investigative service was established. Allan Pinkerton formed his agency because law enforcement agencies in the United States at that time were not able to cope with the rising crime problem. In fact, Pinkerton was able to offer something that no law enforcement agency at that time could offer: nationwide investigative coverage by his detectives. It was not until 1924, with the establishment of the Federal Bureau of Investigation, that any law enforcement agency could equal Pinkerton's scope and size of operation.

When President Abraham Lincoln was elected, Pinkerton became aware of a plot to kidnap the president-elect on his way to Washington, DC, between Harrisburg, Pennsylvania, and Maryland. In a meeting in Harrisburg, Pinkerton advised Lincoln of this plot and secretly escorted Lincoln to Washington, DC, where the president-elect was later sworn into office. During the Civil War, Pinkerton provided a valuable service to the United States by organizing the first Secret Service to stop the counterfeiting of U.S. currency by the Confederates and collecting intelligence on behalf of the U.S. government. In essence, Pinkerton was providing homeland security for the United States.

After the Civil War, the Pinkerton agency continued to provide professional service to the private sector nationwide. Pinkerton detectives brought down the Molly Maguires in Pennsylvania and tracked down bank and train robbers in the West. Pinkerton created the "Ten Most Wanted" list and hired the first female investigators. Pinkerton's agency still exists today.

## The Early 1900s

At the turn of the century, with the increase in industrial development in the United States, private investigative agencies began to flourish. Some, like the Burns Detective Agency, which was formed in 1909, competed with Pinkerton and provided nationwide coverage. However, the majority of the private investigative services were individual or small agencies that provided localized service to businesses to protect their assets and conduct internal investigations. Much of the work rivaled that of law enforcement agencies of that time period. During the 1920s and 1930s, federal, state, and local law enforcement agencies began to expand and develop into professional organizations. The role of the private investigator continued to expand during this period offering service to the private sector.

## Post–World War II Development of Private Investigation

In the late 1940s and 1950s, there was an increase in the number of small or one-person agencies. Investigative cases handled by these agencies included divorce and other domestic matters. Private investigators also provided legal and criminal defense investigations for the legal community, and internal theft and counterespionage investigations to the business community.

During this time period, legislation was introduced in some states to establish requirements for the licensing of private investigators. The Commonwealth of Pennsylvania was the first state to introduce such legislation for the licensing of private investigators. The Pennsylvania Private Detective Act of 1953 required any individual or corporation seeking to provide investigative or security services such as body guards and security officers to be licensed. The licensing requirement is that the applicant(s) is a partnership or corporation, have no criminal record, and be bonded. It also states that the applicant have at least 3 years of police experience above the rank of patrol officer or have worked as an investigator for a licensed private detective for at least 3 years, and pay the required fee. There is no testing or consideration of educational background with the act. Other states began to pass laws requiring private investigators to be licensed. Today, most states require such licensing.

From the 1960s until 2001, there had been enormous growth in the private investigation profession and the diverse services offered by private investigators across the United States and globally. The types of investigations have expanded to include workplace ethics, fraud, and preemployment and general background investigations.

## Post–9/11: The Role of Private Investigation in Support of Homeland Security

The most devastating terrorist attack to date against the United States of America occurred on September 11, 2001, when Islamic terrorists boarded commercial aircraft, murdered the crew, and hijacked the aircraft. The aircraft were then used as weapons of mass destruction in New York City, Washington, DC, and in Pennsylvania to murder more than 3000 individuals.

The outcome of the events of September 11, 2001, demonstrated the lack of intelligence sharing between federal law enforcement, state and local law enforcement, the intelligence community, and the private security profession. This historic event led to a reorganization of most federal law enforcement and security services into the Department of Homeland Security. It also led to more communication between the newly established Department of Homeland Security, the Federal Bureau of Investigation, the U.S. intelligence community, and the U.S. military, as well as state and local law enforcement. There were also efforts to increase the communication and information sharing between all governmental law enforcement, security, and intelligence agencies with the private security profession. ASIS International (founded as the American Society for Industrial Security) and the International Association of Chiefs of Police along with the Department of Homeland Security and the Federal Bureau of Investigation worked together to improve communication with the private security profession.

To facilitate the participation of the private security profession and the public in protection of the homeland, counterterrorism awareness training programs were developed and grants for local training were provided to the private sector by the Department of Homeland Security. Some nationwide security awareness programs were developed to include the Aircraft Owners and Pilots Association Airport Watch Program for general aviation, the U.S. Coast Guard America's Waterways Watch Program for the maritime community, and the American Trucking Association security awareness program for that modality of transportation.

Within the private security profession, ASIS International and the American Board for Certification in Homeland Security became leaders in providing homeland security and counterterrorism training and certification to the security profession. Colleges and universities now offer degrees in homeland security and specialized areas of security such as a bachelor of science degree in aviation security from Embry-Riddle Aeronautical University Worldwide Campus.

With private investigators being part of the security profession, they can take advantage of the education, training, professional certifications, and information sharing in order to do their part during the performance of their duties in protecting the homeland. One never knows when what appears to be a routine private investigation may lead as it relates to homeland security.

Private investigators are also hired by government agencies to conduct background investigations for sensitive positions and those seeking governmental security clearances in government service or working with private industry contractors. Private investigators may also conduct counterespionage and counterterrorism investigations for private security. The private investigator plays a vital role within the security profession and protection of the homeland.

# Bibliography

Benny, D. J. *The Private Investigator's Professional Reference*. Billingham: International Foundation for Protection Officers, 1993.

Doyle, A. C. *The Adventures of Sherlock Holmes*. London: Harper Brothers, 1892.

Mackay, J. *Allan Pinkerton: The First Private Eye*. New York: John Wiley & Sons, 1997.

*Chapter 2*

# Private Investigation Licensing Requirements

## State Private Investigation Licensing Requirements and Fees

There are no national or federal private investigator licenses that will allow an individual to operate as an investigator in all 50 states. In most states, a professional license is required for an individual to operate as a private investigator or to operate a private investigative agency. It is important to check the current licensing requirements of your particular state. (See Appendix A, "State Licensing for Private Investigators" and Appendix E, "Pennsylvania Private Detective Act.")

Being licensed in one state does not necessarily mean that the license can be utilized in other states. In fact, most states do not have reciprocal agreements. In addition to state requirements, there may also be local laws regulating the operation of an investigative business, so it is important check with your local government to ensure that those requirements are met.

The fee for a private investigator license varies from state to state, which can range from $50 to $500 for a private investigator license for a 1- to 5-year licensing period. Fees may vary, depending on the type of business, be it a sole proprietary, partnership, or corporation.

## Required Experience, Residency, and Age

Most states require experience for one to be licensed as a private investigator. The requirement ranges from 2 to 5 years of work experience as an investigator with a current license holder or as a local, state, federal, or military law enforcement officer, investigator, or special agent.

Some states require that the applicant be a resident of that state for a period of time before applying for the private investigator license. The residency requirement can range from 1 to 5 years.

All states that license private investigators have a minimum age requirement; the minimum age requirements in most states range from 21 to 25 years of age.

## Required Education, Training, and Examinations

Educational standards, if any, are generally not high. A high school diploma or GED certificate is the only requirement in some states. Some states may require a college degree or college credits in a related course of study such as security administration, criminal justice, or homeland security from an accredited college or university.

Some states have mandatory security certification programs that an applicant must complete before being licensed. The course requirements can range from one day to several weeks. Some states require passing of a written and/or oral examination to obtain a private investigator license. Such an examination may be part of a state mandatory training program or may just be a singular process of taking an examination on private investigation. (See Appendix G, "Virginia Private Investigator Training Course Outline.")

## Insurance and Bonding

Insurance coverage is usually optional in most states. If it is not a legal requirement for licensing, it is highly recommended that the investigator carry liability insurance for protection from legal action for errors or omissions. This is even more important if the private investigator is carrying a firearm and taking part in protective service operations for clients. It is a very litigious society in which the private investigator operates, and the private investigator needs to be protected from such risk. Having such liability insurance is also an excellent marketing tool.

Nearly all states require that the private investigator be bonded. The amount of the bond ranges from $5000 to $20,000. The bond is assigned to the governmental authority issuing the private investigator license. Should the private investigator violate the restriction set forth in the license, the government agency can then collect on the private investigator bond.

## Background Investigations

All states require the private investigator applicant to undergo an extensive background investigation. The investigation is completed by a government licensing agency or law enforcement agency, such as the state police. The background investigation may include a criminal records check, credit check, personal references, and employment and general educational histories. If a certification course or testing is a requirement, that will also be verified. Insurance or bonding requirements will also be verified where applicable.

## Bibliography

Benny, D. J. *The Private Investigator's Professional Reference.* Billingham: International Foundation for Protection Officers, 1993.

Fischer, R. J. and G. Green. *Introduction to Security.* 9th ed. Burlington, MA: Elsevier, 2012.

Kovacich, G. L. and E. P. Halibozek. *The Manager's Handbook for Corporate Security.* Burlington, MA: Elsevier, 2003.

# Chapter 3

# Private Investigation and Legal Issues

## Ethics and Conduct

The professional private investigator is expected to maintain the highest professional and moral standards. The quality of a professional private investigator ultimately depends upon the willingness of the practitioner to observe special standards of conduct and to manifest good faith in professional relationships. According to Timothy J. Walsh and Richard J. Healy, noted security professionals and authors of the *Protection of Assets Manual*, professionalism is "highly competent performance in a field requiring special knowledge and skills."

In nearly all 50 states, an individual must be professionally licensed to operate as a private investigator. Once licensed, the investigator will not succeed if he or she does not possess that special knowledge or skill described by Walsh and Healy. In the field of investigations, an individual must have technical, human, and conceptual skills in the areas of investigation, security, criminal and civil law, business management, marketing, and the ability to communicate with individuals from all sectors of society.

Whether an occupation can be considered to be a profession depends not only on meeting the criteria of requiring specialized skills and knowledge or on being professionally licensed, but also on whether the occupation is accepted as a profession by other professionals and the general public. In order for an occupation to attain professional stature, the practitioners must establish and adhere to standards for operation, training, and ethical conduct. Formal codes of ethics to regulate conduct, such as those established by the World Association of Detectives and ASIS International, are an important part of the process of attaining professional status.

The following Professional Code of Ethics, as established by the World Association of Detectives, is provided with permission.

## Code of Ethics as Members of the World Association of Detectives, Inc.

We share a singular responsibility for maintaining the integrity and trust of the private detective or investigative profession. In discharging this responsibility, we mutually pledge that:

### I

We will endeavour to perform our professional duties in accordance with the highest moral principles.

### II

We will direct our concerted efforts toward the support, advancement, elevation, and furtherance of high personal and professional conduct in the pursuance of business in our own communities, our respective countries, and with our fellow members wherever they may be.

### III

We will strive to strengthen the membership by selecting and approving for membership only those individuals qualified personally and professionally and whose business operations are conducted in an honest and legitimate manner.

### IV

We will be faithful and diligent in carrying out assignments entrusted to us, and to determine the true facts and render honest, unbiased reports in reference thereto.

### V

We will respect the best interests of our clients by maintaining a high standard of performance and reporting to our clients the full facts ascertained as a result of the work and effort expended whether they be advantageous or detrimental to the interest of the client; and that nothing be withheld from the client save by the dictates of law.

## VI

We will at all times perform our duties within the bounds of the law and will not permit nor demand of any employee nor fellow member any violation of the law or any manner of fraud.

## VII

We will labour diligently and unceasingly to elevate the standard of practices of our agency members and will not tolerate unscrupulous invasion of our business contracts with clients by any member who intrudes knowingly and wilfully for his own private advantage or financial gain to the detriment and/or injury of another member.

## VIII

We will promote and protect the interest of our fellow members, and all members of the profession having knowledge of any unlawful or unprofessional practices of any other member shall immediately inform the Association thereof so that disciplinary action may be taken.

## IX

We will further an honest and legitimate manner of operation and will preserve a client's confidence beyond the term of employment of any private detective, investigator, or other employee; and other employment will not be accepted which involves the disclosure or use of the confidences either for the private advantage of the member or his employees, or to the disadvantage of the client without his knowledge and consent, even though there may be other available sources of information.

## X

We will respect the rights of our clients and refrain from divulging information to newspapers or other publications in the protection of our clients and to prevent interference in the administration of justice or a fair trial in the courts.

## XI

We will refrain from using unprofessional media for advertising or by personal communications or interviews that fail to qualify in professional capacity and fidelity to trust.

## XII

We will avoid controversies with fellow members concerning compensation by using some form of written agreement or letter which shall state terms or fees as agreed upon by both parties. At all times, we will remember that the private investigator/detective business is a profession and all financial dealings with clients should be handled on that basis; and that a private detective or investigator should accept no compensation, commission, rebate or other advantage from others without the knowledge and consent of his client. If necessary, we may resort to the courts to prevent injustice, imposition, or fraud.

### XIII

We will promote programs with educational intent designed to raise standards, improve efficiency, and increase effectiveness of the private investigator/detective profession.

### XIV

We will work together toward the achievement of the professional objectives of the Association.

### XV

We will observe strictly the precepts of truth, accuracy and prudence.

ASIS International distinguishes the security professional from the non-security professional.

## ASIS International Professional Code of Ethics

I. Perform professional duties in accordance with the laws and highest moral principles.
II. Observe the precepts of truthfulness, honesty, and integrity.
III. Be faithful and diligent in discharging professional responsibilities.
IV. Be competent in discharging professional responsibilities.
V. Do not maliciously injure the professional reputation of colleagues.

It is important that private investigators perform their duties and conduct themselves in a professional manner. This includes being honest, treating all clients in a fair manner, and conducting investigations in a legal manner. Adhering to the professional ethics of the private investigation profession will distinguish the private investigator as a professional.

## Legal Authority

As discussed under the topic of licensing for private investigators, the private investigator license permits the holder to legally conduct private investigations for a fee charged to the clients who hire the private investigator. Investigators may also advertise such services and promote their profession.

Being licensed as a private investigator does not give the holder of such a license any special law enforcement authority or access to law enforcement information. They may not use their private investigator credentials, be it a photo identification card and/or a metal badge or shield, depending on the state licensing requirements for what the private investigator is issued, to imply or infer that they have law enforcement authority or are a law enforcement agent.

Being a licensed private investigator does not permit the holder of the license to have access to individual privacy information. The private investigator only has access to public records, just as any other citizen would have. The private investigator does not have any special arrest authority. Based on the type of work conducted by private investigators, they should not have a need to make an arrest. If violations of the law are observed, the private investigator can report such activity to the local law enforcement agency for legal action.

## Carrying Firearms

Where authorized by law and with a concealed carry license, firearms may be carried by the private investigator. Many states require specialized training before being authorized to carry a firearm. In Pennsylvania, for example, a private investigator or security officer who carries a baton or firearm must complete what is known as the Lethal Weapons Act 235 Course. To attend the 40-hour course, the private investigator must submit to a criminal background check, as well as medical and psychology evaluations. The course covers the legal aspects of carrying a weapon, the authority of a security officer, use-of-force considerations, and the Pennsylvania Crimes Code. Students must pass a written test and qualify on the firing range to become certified under the Lethal Weapons Act. It is important to know the requirements with regard to carrying a weapon in the state in which a private investigator is operating to ensure compliance with the laws of the state.

Firearms may be carried by the private investigator based on the legal requirements of the state in which they operate. The threat and assignment that the private investigator is engaged in must also be considered. It is the professional view of the author that the private investigator should be armed if authorized by law for their protection and support of homeland security. It is the author's professional view that the more individuals legally carrying a firearm, the safer the country is from terrorism and traditional violent crime.

It is vital for license holders to understand that when they are traveling in or through another state, they are subject to the firearms laws of that state. The private investigator needs to check the state law for reciprocity of the conceal carry license they hold, to ensure they can legally carry a concealed weapon into the state they wish to travel. Even if the private investigator is authorized to carry a concealed weapon in another state, the private investigator needs to make sure that the weapon, magazine capacity, and ammunition they have is legal in the state they seek to carry the firearm, as it may differ from the state in which they operate each day.

A private investigator most often will carry a revolver or semiautomatic firearm as shown in Figures 3.1 and 3.2.

In addition to state legal requirements for qualification and certification to carry a concealed firearm, the private investigator should be trained and qualify with the weapons and ammunition they carry at least once a year. The private investigator who carries firearms should also be trained in the situational use of force so that there is an understanding by the private investigator when deadly force with a firearm may be used. This training and qualification is to ensure that the private investigator is proficient in the use of the weapon and circumstances in which such weapons may legally be used so that the private investigator acts in a professional manner and is less likely to be exposed to civil or criminal action. (See Appendix F, "Pennsylvania Lethal Weapons Training Act.")

**Figure 3.1  Walther P-38.9mm, Beretta 9mm, and Walther PPK .380 semiautomatic pistols. (Photograph by Daniel J. Benny.)**

**Figure 3.2 Smith & Wesson .357 revolver and .38 revolver. (Photograph by Daniel J. Benny.)**

## Liability Issues

It is a very litigious society in which the private investigator operates. This creates a risk for the private investigator should the investigator make a mistake or a perceived mistake during the performance of their duties for a client. This could lead to civil litigation against the private investigator for damages that could be devastating to the private investigator's reputation and business.

Some of the common causes of civil action against the private investigator include defamation should any untrue information be said about an individual during an investigation. Legal action can also be taken against an investigator for violation of individual constitutional rights of privacy or discrimination. A release of improper information related to a client could be a cause for civil action against the private investigator. A client can bring action for errors and omissions that may occur during an investigation. Other more serious tort actions against the private investigator include false arrest, excessive use of force, and use of deadly force with a firearm or other protective devices such as a baton. These serious tort actions may also lead to criminal action against the private investigator.

The important fact to remember concerning successful litigation against the private investigator is that the investigator must have performed their duties in an inappropriate manner that caused damage to an individual or organization. There are of course fraudulent lawsuits that may occur even if the investigator did nothing wrong. Because of this litigation risk, it is important that the private investigator has liability insurance even if it is not a requirement of the state in which they are licensed and operate. The liability insurance should cover the investigator for all activity in which they provide service for their clients. If the private investigator carries a firearm during the course of their professional duties, special firearms coverage is recommended. There are many insurance companies that provide special insurable coverage for private investigators to include the carrying of firearms. The individual private investigator or sole proprietor may consider additional firearms concealed carry insurance from the U.S. Concealed Carry Association or U.S. Law Shield. These organizations specializes in insurance and legal services in firearms-related incidents. They offer a 24/7 emergency call line for immediate attorney assistance for any incident involving the discharge of a firearm and ongoing legal counsel by attorneys who specialize in firearms defense cases.

Liability insurance is vital to ensure that the investigator is protected from any civil action related to the performance of the professional services they offer. The type and amount of coverage is based on the services offered by the investigator and the risk associated with such services. In some states, state law may mandate the type of liability insurance and the amount of coverage and investigator must carry.

## Bibliography

Fischer, R. J. and G. Green. *Introduction to Security*. 9th ed. Burlington, MA: Elsevier, 2012.
Kovacich, G. L. and E. P. Halibozek. *The Manager's Handbook for Corporate Security*. Burlington, MA: Elsevier, 2003.

# Chapter 4

# Establishing a Professional Private Investigative Business

## Branding the Investigative Business

Making a decision on the name of the investigative business is one of the primary and most important decisions one needs to make when establishing a private investigation business. It is the branding that will be used to market the business. In order to complete an application for a private investigator license, one will need to state the name of the business. This may be an individual's name or a fictitious business name. The name selected will have an impact on how the business is perceived by potential clients and may very well have a role in determining the types of clients that are attracted to the private investigative business. The position in which the investigative business is listed in the telephone book online professional directories will hinge on which letter of the alphabet the name of the private investigative business begins with.

There are some private investigators, such as the author, who utilize their own name. This can be an excellent selling point that stresses personalized service in attracting clients. A fictitious private investigative business name is often used; this is especially true in the case of corporations. The use of a fictitious name allows the private investigative firm to establish an image of what the private investigative organization is to be. The name can represent the type of work specialized in and services offered.

The selection of a name of the investigative business is a personal one. What works for one investigator in one city may not work in another. The decision will depend on the image the private investigator wants to portray, the types of investigations to be conducted, and the type of clientele the investigative firm seeks to attract.

## Sole Proprietor, Partnership, Corporation

In most states, there are three types of private investigative businesses that can be established. These include a sole proprietary, partnership, or corporation. The sole proprietary investigative business is one in which the license is in the owner's name. The investigative business may have other employees, such as investigators and administrative staff, but it is usually small. One advantage of this type of an operation is that the owner is in control of the business. The private investigative license usually costs less for a sole proprietor than a partnership or corporation. Another advantage is that the investigative business can be marketed as having a personalized touch. The disadvantages are that the owner has all of the responsibility and because the organization is usually small, it may result in limited growth potential of the investigative organization.

In a partnership, two or more individuals join together to form the private investigative business. The benefit to this type of arrangement is that the costs, workload, and responsibility are shared among the partners. This is also conducive to the expansion of the private investigative organization. The disadvantage is that each individual partner will not have total control of the private investigative business.

Private investigative firms may also be established and licensed as a corporation. Establishing a corporation takes time and requires a more substantial investment for the license fee, attorney's fees, and the costs associated with establishing the articles of incorporation. The final results can be beneficial because the private investigative firm will portray an image of being a larger organization and be in a position where the individual owners will have more protection from personal liability.

## Office Location

The establishment of an office site is a consideration that needs to be addressed. Office space can be rented or purchased as part of a commercial property, or the private investigator can be based out of their residence. Most private investigative agencies will rent or buy commercial space. In most cases, the sole proprietor private investigator will operate from their residence; there is no need to spend money for commercial space when the private investigator can utilize an in-house office. Most investigative work does not result from walk-in clients. Clients will usually contact the investigator by telephone having learned about the investigative business through the investigator's web page, directory listings, a referral, or previous contacts. The use of a home office saves office rental costs and allows for the deduction of office space in the home for tax purposes. A post office (PO) box address can be used so that the actual street location is unknown. Clients can be contacted by phone and e-mail. Clients can be met at their office or at a public location.

# Determining the Market, Services Offered, and Fees

There are unlimited sources of clients in the private investigative profession. Some private investigators specialize in specific investigative work, while others will take on any category of investigation. This decision whether to specialize in an investigation category should be based on the investigator's experience, expertise, and interest. The competition and the size and nature of the city in which the private investigator operates will also have a bearing on such a decision. It is the author's professional opinion that unless a private investigator has cornered the market on a specialized service in his or her area, it is best to be flexible and work a variety of types of cases for which the investigator is qualified. The areas may be explored for potential clients based on the area in which the private investigator is operating.

# Current and Past Clients

One of the most effective means of obtaining clients is through the personal referral of a current or past client. They can attest to the private investigator's professionalism and make a first-account recommendation. The private investigator should provide extra business cards to clients and encourage them to make recommendations to friends or associates who might need their services now or in the future.

# Other Private Investigators

Many private investigators, because they specialize in one specific area or operate independently, might need assistance in their local area from time to time. Although the investigative business is competitive, it is important that private investigators network and be available to assist one another on cases. Private investigators living in other cities, states, or countries may also seek the services of a private investigator to obtain information or conduct an investigation in a particular area. Belonging to professional, state, and private investigative organizations as well as national and international organizations such as the World Association of Detectives or the Association of British Investigators and being listed in national private investigative directories will increase the chances of obtaining work from other private investigators globally.

## Private Individuals

For some private investigators, a majority of their work is attributed to private individuals. Private clients, although not always the most profitable for the investigator, will often provide some of the more interesting assignments. Investigations requested will range from domestic surveillance to the location of missing persons. It may include the investigation of theft or protective service.

## Legal Profession

Working as a private investigator or legal investigator for the legal profession can be one of the most rewarding investigative experiences, both professionally and financially. Investigations in this area include criminal defense, accident investigations, personal injury, or domestic litigation. Independent attorneys and large law firms are both potential sources of clients.

Contacts with attorneys can be made through a search of the internet or telephone directory, which is then followed by personal contact, direct mailing or e-mailing. Scanning the newspaper on a daily basis allows you to identify attorneys who are representing individuals facing criminal charges and can provide a lead on a potential client.

Other sources of legal clients include local legal bar associations or professional legal groups that maintain lists of private investigators for referral to attorneys. In many areas, the public defender's office will utilize or refer private investigators for use on criminal cases.

## Corporations

The utilization of private investigators in the private sector is increasing each year. With the concern of reduced profits and increasing competition, internal theft, and industrial espionage, corporations are looking for ways to reduce their risk and losses and to increase their assets. Private investigators are being utilized to conduct investigations involving internal theft, corruption, industrial espionage, fraud, ethics violations, workplace violence, and drugs in the workplace. This may take the form of either an overt or a covert investigation. With the increased competition in the job market, employers in the corporate sector are becoming concerned that the individual they select for a position is the best for the position and in fact has the credentials they claim. The private investigator is being utilized to perform preemployment background investigations on candidates, as well as updated background checks on current employees who are being considered for promotion or are being given new responsibilities in a sensitive area of the corporation.

The investigator who offers services in the areas of protective service, electronic countermeasures, and security consulting are in demand by corporations who are developing or expanding their security programs, especially those who are concerned with the increased threat of terrorism and the issues of homeland security.

## Commercial Businesses

Commercial or retail businesses, such as retail stores, fast-food chains, service stations, and movie theaters, utilize private investigators to conduct preemployment investigations, theft and fraud investigations, and undercover assignments. A specialized service that might be offered to the commercial establishment is the shopping service. This type of investigation includes the private investigator going undercover to determine if there is evidence of employee wrongdoing and to evaluate the service to the customer. The investigator conducting a shopping service should be alert to potential safety hazards, such as poor housekeeping, inaccessible fire doors, and blocked fire extinguishers.

## Cultural Properties

Cultural properties face many threats related to theft of artifacts, works of art, books, and documents. They may also be a symbolic terrorist target based on the nature of the cultural property and where it is located. The private investigator may be called upon to investigate a theft of cultural property, preemployment investigation, or internal ethics or policy investigations. Security consulting services may also be provided to such institutions that are considered a soft and often a symbolic target of terrorism.

## Maritime Community

The maritime community is comprised of many entities, including marines, ports, and watercraft. The watercraft include small pleasure craft, yachts, and commercial and military ships. The maritime domain serves as a critical waterways highway for the global economy. This environment presents unique security challenges encompassing vast oceans, coastal and inland waterways, commercial shipping lanes, and countless ports of entry. According to the U.S. Department of Homeland Security, the United States has 95,000 miles of coastline, 361 ports, to include 8 of the world's 50 highest-volume ports, and 10,000 miles of navigable waterways. This vast industry provides the opportunity for the private investigator in areas of theft, fraud, and policy investigations. Counterterrorism investigations are of value for

**Figure 4.1    The author's 1964 Boston Whaler. (Photograph by Daniel J. Benny.)**

this industry. Security consulting and protective service assignment are other services that could be offered (Figure 4.1).

## General Aviation

General aviation airports are used exclusively by general aviation aircraft. These airports do not offer commercial air carrier service. The airports might be privately owned by an individual, family, or corporation. General aviation aircraft are fixed-wing or rotary aircraft that are used for the private transport of individuals, company staff or guests, and cargo. Individuals might own a general aviation aircraft such as a Cessna (Figure 4.2). People can also rent general aviation aircraft from a local general aviation airport for the pleasure of flying and to travel on weekends and holidays. General aviation aircraft also include aircraft utilized by corporations to transport staff, executives, and customers of the organization.

General aviation is critical to the security, infrastructure, and economic success of the United States. It supports many aspects of society. This includes public safety, business, agriculture, commercial airports, aeronautical education, and many aspects of the aviation profession. General aviation also serves as a valuable recreational activity to thousands of general aviation pilots and aircraft owners who utilize general aviation airports and fixed-base operation facilities across the United States. Aviation is the target of crime and terrorism, so the private investigator

**Figure 4.2    The author's 1961 Cessna C-150. (Photograph by Daniel J. Benny.)**

could aid in homeland security by providing investigative, security consultant, and counterterrorism services to the general aviation community. Traditional pre-employment, theft, and fraud investigations can also be performed by the private investigator upon request.

## Government Agencies

The private investigator may be asked to conduct investigations for governmental agencies, directly contributing to homeland security. Numerous federal agencies, such as the Defense Security Service, the Office of Personnel Management, and even the Federal Bureau of Investigation contract private investigators to perform routine background investigations related to government security clearances. As funding becomes even tighter, it is expected that other agencies will also seek the services of private investigators.

Throughout the country, state agencies utilize private investigators to perform a variety of functions. Investigative assignments may include preemployment background checks, security consulting, or assignments with a special prosecutor investigating government corruption, ethics, or agency regulation and policy violations.

Local government agencies also use the services of private investigators. Many local courts utilize investigators for pretrial investigations for a public defender's office. Local civil service commissions are another source of work in providing background investigations on potential police officers or other public employees.

## Insurance Companies

Insurance companies provide numerous work opportunities for the private investigator. Workers' compensation claims and accident and injury investigations comprise the majority of this work. Insurance companies also contract for preemployment and background investigations related to various matters they may be dealing with.

## Rates and Fees

There are no legal limits on what a private investigator can charge; rates are based on the local market. A private investigator's rate will depend on their location and competition. Most investigators charge their clients an hourly rate. The current national average is $60 per hour. This hourly rate includes time for travel, conducting the investigation, and the writing of reports. If court testimony is required of the private investigator, the same hourly rates are charged for the court time.

In addition to hourly rates, the client is charged for expenses. These expenses may include vehicle gas, parking, and photocopying or other imaging charges. The private investigator can also charge a per diem to cover the cost of meals and lodging required during the course of the investigation.

Some private investigators establish a flat fee for a specific service that they charge the client. Examples might include $60 to conduct a criminal records check or $50 for a property search. A flat fee or discounted rate may also be given to clients who provide steady work.

The strategic issue is to establish a rate that is competitive with the local market area. A private investigator who overcharges may well send potential clients to other private investigators. The private investigator should not set their fee too low. If rates are set too low, it will lower the standard fee of the local area for all private investigators.

## Marketing the Business

### *Advertising and Publicity*

Without advertising and publicity, potential clients will not be aware of the private investigative services that are provided. It is important that advertising be cost effective. The private investigator just starting in business does not need to invest enormous resources to advertise, but some effort must be made to obtain clients. There are many basic forms of advertising, which are essential, but there is also the potential for an enormous amount of free advertisement through publicity.

Licensed-Bonded-Insured
Limited Liability Company
Established 1981

# Dr. Daniel J. Benny
### Private Investigator & Security Consultant

202 Valley Road-Bellevue Park     Office     717 238-1740
Harrisburg, Pennsylvania 17104-1430     Facsimile     717 238-1741
DrBennyPI @comcast.net     Mobile     717 574-9273
WWW.BennyPI.com

**Figure 4.3 Sample business card.**

## Business Cards

The most essential and cost-effective form of advertising is the business card (Figure 4.3). These are relatively inexpensive and can be passed out by the handful. Business cards can be given to virtually anyone the private investigator meets under any circumstances, be it business or social. The business card will inform the individual or organization of the private investigator. Business cards can be distributed during personal contacts with prospective clients, as well as through direct mailing. Many public areas and businesses have bulletin boards where business cards may be posted and displayed. Take advantage of this cost-effective form of advertising and distribute as many as possible.

## Internet Web Pages and Social Media

It is essential for a private investigator to be connected on the Internet with a web page and profiles on social media sites such as LinkedIn and Facebook. Most potential clients will go to the Internet. By having a professional web page the private investigator can be connected to the potential client. The private investigator can also establish a Facebook business page that will link to the official business web page.

The web page should include the history of the investigator or firm, location, phone number, e-mail, and services provided. The more information that one can provide on a professional website will attract clients.

## Local Telephone Directory

A listing in the local telephone directory years ago was the lifeblood of the private investigative business. The majority of prospective clients now will look online. Some individuals and organizations will still utilize the Yellow Pages of the local telephone directory for a private investigator to provide the services they require. Most Yellow Pages throughout the country provide two headings under which you can be listed: detective agencies and investigators. This is obviously redundant and is to the financial benefit of the directory. It does, however, require a decision on the part of the investigator as to where to place the ad. Those who can afford to may place advertising under both headings. Having conducted an informal random telephone survey including both private individuals and businesses, the results show that most potential clients seeking a private investigator will look under the heading of investigator.

The size of the advertisement depends on the amount of money the private investigator wants to spend. The decision should be based on local competition and the location of the ad in the alphabetical listing. If the private investigator is the only listing in the local directory, a small one-line ad would be all that is required. An alphabetical listing that allows your ad to be one of the first listings is advantageous since most potential clients simply start at the top of the list. If the private investigator is faced with considerable competition in the local directory, the private investigator will need a larger ad to draw attention to your business.

## National Directories

Having the private investigation business listed in national online private investigative and security directories can be an asset. This will allow the private investigator to reach potential clients throughout the United States and globally who are seeking the services of a private investigator in a specific area or with a special skill.

## Membership Directories

Professional membership is of value to private investigators in selling their image, education, and making professional contacts. Most professional private investigative and security organizations have an online or hard copy membership directory. It may be open to the public or just the members of the professional organization. In any event, this will allow the private investigator to reach potential clients throughout the United States and globally who are seeking the services of a private investigator in a specific area or with a special skill that can be utilized by a client.

## Brochures and Direct Mailings

In order to provide a more in-depth overview of the private investigator's credentials and the services offered, in addition to a web page the development of a professional brochure is recommended. The key elements of the brochure should include specific services offered, experience, educational credentials, and professional memberships, in addition to how a client may contact the private investigator. These brochures may be given directly to potential clients or can be sent out as a direct mailing or PDF e-mail.

The use of direct mailing is not the most cost-effective form of advertising, especially if brochures are sent randomly by the U.S. Postal Service. Most businesses receive enormous amounts of junk mail and spam e-mail, and the private investigator's brochures could easily find themselves filed in the circular container or deleted from an online spam folder. Brochures are more effective when combined with direct personal contact such as a phone call.

## Newspapers

Advertising in daily or weekly newspapers can be an excellent method of obtaining clients. Such advertising is usually expensive for the limited time of exposure. It is, however, one method of getting the word out about the private investigative business.

## Television and Radio

Television and radio advertising can reach a large audience, more than print media. Due to the high costs of airtime, it is not the most cost-effective form of advertising for the private investigator. Based on funding, it may be a method of promoting the private investigative business.

## Free Publicity

The best form of advertising is free advertising. The opportunities to make the services of the private investigator known are unlimited. If the private investigator is good at speaking, dealing with the media, or has writing skills, they can cash in on this free publicity. The private investigator can take advantage of these opportunities by speaking at meetings of professional, public service, and social organizations. Teaching part time at a college or university can be of value. Take advantage of any writing talent by writing letters to the editor, or writing articles for the local newspaper or professional journals and magazines. If you are comfortable speaking with the media, there may be opportunities to appear on local radio or television shows, or to participate in interviews with the local newspaper reporters developing articles on the topic of private investigators.

# Private Investigative Forms

A necessary step in establishing an investigative business is the selection of investigative forms. It is best to keep it simple. What a potential or current client sees when they receive a report is a direct reflection of the private investigator.

There are two categories of business forms the private investigator will need for the investigative business. The first are administrative forms that any business would require, including ledgers, receipts, and time cards. It is neither necessary nor cost effective to have these forms printed specifically for the business. These can be purchased commercially with the private investigator's name and logo imprinted on them.

# Dr. Daniel J. Benny

### Private Investigator & Security Consultant

**Licensed • Bonded • Insured**
Limited Liability Company
Established 1981

Doctor of Philosophy in Criminal Justice
Certified Protection Professional • Professional Certified Investigator
Certified Fraud Examiner • Certified Confidentiality Officer
Certified Aviation Security Professional • Certified Maritime Security Professional
Certified Institutional Protection Manager

202 Valley Road-Bellevue Park    Office (717) 238-1740
Harrisburg, PA 17104-1430    Facsimile (717) 238-1741
DrBennyPI@comcast.net; www.BennyPI.com    Mobile (717) 574-9273

#### SERVICE AGREEMENT

This agreement, entered into on this ___ day ___ 2017 by and between Dr. Daniel J. Benny, a professionally licensed, bonded, insured, Private Investigator & Security Consultant, Limited Liability Company, in accordance with the laws of the Commonwealth of Pennsylvania hereinafter called agent and ____ hereinafter called client.

The client engages the services of agent to conduct an investigation and pay to the agent the fee of $80 per hour. The client also agrees to pay the agent expenses that may be incurred in the performance of the investigation to include mileage in the amount of $0.50 per mile. The taking of depositions and court testimony shall be considered part of the investigative service and payable at the same hourly rate and any travel or lodging expense required for such testimony. The client agrees to pay the agent a retainer fee of $500 in advance. The client understands that additional fees will be required to continue the investigation should the agent's hourly fee and expense exceed the initial retainer. The agent agrees that the client and all information derived from the investigation will be kept confidential and only disseminated to the client or to other parties directed by the client.

The agent reserves the right to cancel this investigative agreement at any time upon written or oral notice to the client and receive full payment for any service rendered and expenses incurred prior to the cancellation. The agent agrees to cancel this investigative agreement at any time upon written or oral notice from the client and receive full payment for any service rendered and expenses incurred prior to the cancellation. Upon cancellation of this agreement any funds not utilized will be returned to the client.

The client agrees and understands that the agent will perform the investigation according to his own methods, in accordance with professional standards and federal, state, and local laws. The client understands that the agent does not guarantee the desired results from the investigation.

The client, or the client's heirs, beneficiaries, devisees, administrators, and assigns further agree to indemnify and hold harmless the agent from any and all actions, claims, damages, and demands of whatever type and wherever situated arising directly or indirectly from the investigation requested by the client.

Client_____    Agent_____

**Figure 4.4    A sample service agreement between a private investigator and client.**

The second type, are forms that are related to the investigative field. These forms will need to be developed to meet specific needs. They can be produced commercially or by the private investigator on a personal computer. The following is a sampling of the basic investigative forms needed.

## *Professional Investigative Service Agreement*

It is important to have a service agreement between the private investigator and client (Figure 4.4). This will ensure that there are no misunderstandings between the private investigator and the client as to rates, the investigation to be conducted, and operating procedures. This form will also be invaluable should litigation ensue with regard to payment of funds.

## *Voluntary Statement*

A Voluntary Statement form will aid in the taking of statements during an investigation and should indicate that the statement is being given voluntarily, without threats or promises (Figure 4.5).

## Dr. Daniel J. Benny

**Private Investigator & Security Consultant**

**Licensed • Bonded • Insured**
Limited Liability Company
Established 1981

Doctor of Philosophy in Criminal Justice
Certified Protection Professional • Professional Certified Investigator
Certified Fraud Examiner • Certified Confidentiality Officer
Certified Aviation Security Professional • Certified Maritime Security Professional
Certified Institutional Protection Manager

202 Valley Road-Bellevue Park      Office (717) 238-1740
Harrisburg, PA 17104-1430       Facsimile (717) 238-1741
DrBennyPI@comcast.net; www.BennyPI.com      Mobile (717) 574-9273

**VOLUNTARY STATEMENT**

I, _____, of _____
make the following voluntary statement to Dr. Daniel J. Benny, Private Investigator & Security Consultant, Limited
Liability Company, on this _____ day of _____, 20___ ,
of my own free will without threats or promises extended to me.

Page ___ of ___

**Figure 4.5  A Voluntary Statement form.**

# Dr. Daniel J. Benny

### Private Investigator & Security Consultant

**Licensed • Bonded • Insured**
Limited Liability Company
Established 1981

Doctor of Philosophy in Criminal Justice
Certified Protection Professional • Professional Certified Investigator
Certified Fraud Examiner • Certified Confidentiality Officer
Certified Aviation Security Professional • Certified Maritime Security Professional
Certified Institutional Protection Manager

202 Valley Road-Bellevue Park    Office (717) 238-1740
Harrisburg, PA 17104-1430    Facsimile (717) 238-1741
DrBennyPI@comcast.net; www.BennyPI.com    Mobile (717) 574-9273

AUTHORIZATION TO RELEASE INFORMATION AND RECORDS

I, _____, hereby authorize Dr. Daniel J. Benny, Private Investigator & Security Consultant, Limited Liability Company, to make inquiries with regard to my background and to examine and/or obtain copies of any or all records pertaining to employment, credit and financial status, criminal records, police reports, military records, educational records, driving records, insurance records, telephone records, business and personal references, and medical and doctors' records.

_____
Signature

_____
Date

**Figure 4.6   An Authorization to Release Information and Records form.**

## *Authorization to Release Information and Records*

An Authorization to Release Information and Records form authorizes the release of all information regarding the individual signing it that will be needed to conduct a preemployment or background investigation (Figure 4.6).

## Equipment

When establishing a private investigative business, one needs to plan equipment needs. Some basic recommended office equipment includes a telephone, an answering machine, a fax machine, a personal computer, a printer/photocopier, a paper shredder, a desk, and a secure filing cabinet for case files. In addition to standard office equipment, specialized investigative equipment may be required. The type of equipment needed will depend on the type of work being conducted. This equipment may include photographic and video cameras, tape recorders, evidence collection tools and containers, protective equipment, polygraph, electronic countermeasures equipment, and first aid or emergency items. Investigative equipment can be purchased locally or from nationwide distributors online.

The following are some sources for private investigative equipment:

- Galls: www.galls.com
- PI Gear: www.pigear.com
- PI Mall: www.pimall.com/nais/equ.find.html
- Sirchie: www.sirchie.com

Manufacturers and distributors may also be located through the annual *Security Management Buyers Guide* published by ASIS International, 1625 Prince Street, Alexandria, VA 22314; www.asisonline.org.

## Bibliography

Benny, D. J. *The Private Investigator's Professional Reference.* Billingham: International Foundation for Protection Officers, 1993.

Doyle, A. C. *The Adventures of Sherlock Holmes.* London: Harper Brothers, 1892.

Fischer, R. J. and G. Green. *Introduction to Security.* 9th ed. Burlington, MA: Elsevier, 2012.

Kovacich, G. L. and E. P. Halibozek. *The Manager's Handbook for Corporate Security.* Burlington, MA: Elsevier, 2003.

# Chapter 5

# Conducting Investigations Related to Homeland Security

There are many different types of investigations that a private investigator may conduct that will be related to homeland security. Some private investigators specialize in specific types of investigations, and other private investigators generalize and take on many different types of investigations. The type of investigations that are provided need to be based on the private investigator's experience, education, interests, and clientele. No matter what the investigation, it will be important to the client, but it may also be important to homeland security. Not all types of investigations that the private investigator may conduct for clients will be discussed in this chapter. The investigations that are common to the private investigator that may have homeland security implications will be explored. The private investigator should have a thorough knowledge of research techniques, surveillance techniques, interviewing techniques, private investigative industry-specific equipment, and know how to collect and preserve evidence. It is also imperative that private investigators understand how to take proper and complete notes. All of these areas will be discussed in this chapter.

## Investigative Methods

Criminal investigations may include work for private individuals on a variety of private matters. It may also include working for the criminal defense in order to determine the true facts of the case to the benefit of the client. Criminal defense investigations involve assisting clients charged with various criminal offenses ranging from homicide to driving under the influence of alcohol. In the criminal investigation, the investigator works closely with the attorney in all aspects of the case.

The client who is a victim of a criminal act might hire a private investigator so as not involve law enforcement authorities. The client might think that the local police department did not perform an adequate investigation of the case. Governmental agencies often retain private investigators or law enforcement agencies to conduct independent criminal investigations, especially in matters involving ethics violations and the corruption of public officials.

When conducting the investigation, the concepts of inductive and deductive reasoning should be applied. Inductive reasoning is observing a set of characteristics based on a premise of broad generalizations and statistical analysis, which leads to the development of a hypothesis. Deductive reasoning is observing a set of characteristics that may be reasoned from a convergence of physical and behavioral actions or patterns within an event or a series of events, such as a crime or series of crimes.

In order to successfully conduct criminal investigations, the private investigator should have an understanding and working knowledge of the theories of inductive and deductive reasoning. This concept has been a valuable tool in the investigation profession for more than 120 years. The theory has been utilized in the investigation of traditional criminal offenses such as robbery, theft, fraud, and burglary. It has also been extensively used in the investigation of criminal profiling of serial killers, sexual predators, drug dealers, organized crime, and, as seen since September 11, 2001, suspected members of international and national terrorist organizations.

The most recognized and famous use of the concept of inductive and deductive reasoning is in the works of Sir Arthur Conan Doyle in the Sherlock Holmes canon of novels and short stories, which first appeared in 1892. Sherlock Holmes utilized these theories to not only solve crime but to build a profile of an individual based on observations of the facts and then to construct a hypothesis around the facts. Holmes used these methods in the investigation of tradition crime, espionage, and in the protection of the English homeland.

Inductive reasoning is the use of an inference that is established through a set of observations leading to a generalization, which is known as a premise. Observation is a key element of all investigations. A singular fact may be the difference in the outcome of an investigation. As Sherlock Holmes states, "You know my method. It is founded upon the observation of trifles." The premise is a working assumption. Although a working assumption has been established, it does not mean that it is an automatically valid assumption.

The inductive argument or assumption investigates issues in the case from the specific to the general and is known as inductive generalization. A conclusion is formed about observations and characteristics of a single individual or single event. It may also include the characteristics and observations of several individuals or events. Based on this information, a preliminary generalization is made concluding that similar individuals or events that are seen or encountered in the future will exhibit the same observations of the originally documented characteristics.

Deductive reasoning involves the argument that if the premise is true, then the conclusion is also true. Within deductive reasoning, the conclusions are arrived at through the given premises. The reasoning moves from the general to the specific when utilized in a criminal investigation. An offender's behavior and/or patterns could be suggestive of critical offender characteristics.

Deductive reasoning includes looking at a set of characteristics of the offender that are reasoned by the convergence of all of the physical evidence in the case as well as behavioral evidence patterns within that case or a series of related criminal crimes and cases.

Inductive and deductive reasoning can be a valuable tool in criminal investigation and is still taught by reviewing the stories of Sherlock Holmes at the Peel Center, the police training academy for the London Metropolitan Police.

# Interviewing Techniques

In all investigations, the private investigator will be interviewing individuals. This will include the client to gather the facts of the case. It then may include witnesses, sources of information, and the subject of an investigation. Before any interview occurs, the private investigator must first gather as much information on the topic as possible. The private investigator should outline the facts already known. From that outline, the private investigator should identify possible missing information that will need to be obtained during the interview. This will also provide an opportunity to identify information or facts that need corroboration. The goal of the interview is to gather information. If the private investigator makes the proper preparation as to what information is needed, the interview will be more successful.

When a private investigator conducts an interview, even with a possible suspect in the case, the Miranda warning need not be given. It is only required to be given by public law enforcement when interviewing a suspect of a crime. It is not recommended that it be given by a private investigator as the person will only "lawyer up" and not provide any information. With that said, it is best to allow suspects to speak and use it against them in any civil or criminal actions.

When conducting an interview, the private investigator must first present a professional image in order to be successful. Suggestions to keep up this appearance would be for the private investigator to be well groomed and to dress professionally for the occasion. The private investigator should noticeably categorize him- or herself as a professional investigator and show identification of being a licensed private investigator. The interviewee should be made aware of the purpose of the interview. The information provided to the interviewee will depend on the situation and the individual's relationship to the investigation.

Establishing the proper tone at the beginning of the interview is vital. This will vary with the private investigator's professional style and how the private investigator thinks the interviewee might react to that style during the interview. The goal is to make the interviewee at ease and as comfortable as possible so that they can be focused during the interview. The private investigator should explain to the person to be interviewed the protocol for the interview process and how the interview will proceed.

Some methods that can be utilized when conducting the interview include the following:

- Take your time and never establish a timeline for the interview.
- Stay in control and keep the interview focused on the facts of the case.
- All questions asked by the private investigator need to be simple and easy to understand.
- Questions should be open-ended unless the private investigator needs to verify facts of the case or facts already known.
- The private investigator should let the interviewee do most of the talking.
- Listen effectually.
- Listen to find the truth.
- Questions need to be direct when trying to establish the facts.
- Maintain eye contact with the interviewee.
- Utilize feedback for clarification related to answers.

The private investigator needs to be aware that the person being interviewed may need to differentiate between fact and opinion. The information must also be corroborated with a secondary source to be reliable.

During the progression of the interview, the private investigator may be challenged by an individual who exhibits some emotion. The emotion may be fear, frustration, anger, hostility, or even guilt. The individual may arrive at the interview with negative feelings or such feelings may arise during the interview. Feelings can alter the outcome of the interview and prevent finding the true facts of the case. It is advantageous if the private investigator has the ability to recognize such feelings during the interview and is able to respond to them in an effective manner.

# Covert Operations

## Surveillance Methods

In the course of conducting a private investigation, surveillance will often be required. The surveillance will always be covert since the subjects must not know that they are being observed.

The surveillance can be fixed where the private investigator watches a specific location live in person. It may also be a fixed technical surveillance where the private investigator sets up cameras in an unattended vehicle to watch a fixed location for an extended period of time to record events without the private investigator being present.

There is also two- or three-person moving surveillance. This is a team effort to monitor the subject on foot using up to three investigators. It may also be accomplished using up to three vehicles driven by investigators.

The undercover investigation is most often used in the workplace to investigate criminal activity such as theft, fraud, drugs, or smuggling. It may also be used to investigate possible terrorist activity. It can be dangerous for the private investigator.

## Fixed Surveillance

Fixed surveillance is the type of surveillance in which the private investigator observes the target of the investigation, be it an individual or a location or perhaps a vehicle from a fixed location at an effective distance from the target. The surveillance could be conducted by two or more investigators. The use of two investigators is considered more desirable and if possible is the recommended method. This method allows the private investigators to intermittently alter or switch their positions. This will reduce the chance that the subject of the investigation identifies the surveillance. By using only a single private investigator on such an assignment, the investigator may be recognized over a period of time, which could end the surveillance for that period.

## Fixed Technical Surveillance

Stationary technical surveillance is when the private investigator utilizes technical equipment to conduct surveillance at a fixed location. This can include the use of cameras, binoculars, and other monitoring equipment that is legal in the state, location, and manner in which the equipment is being used. For example, the use of a hidden camera for visual recording placed in a parked vehicle. The unattended vehicle should be situated near the surveillance target in a manner and area that would not raise suspicion. By using this method the private investigators can take photographs and videos when the need arises and at any time of the day. This method allows the private investigator to monitor the target for extended hours without having to be at the location for the time that the surveillance is taking place.

## Two- or Three-Person Moving Surveillance

The two- or three-person moving surveillance method is more complex but delivers a more successful outcome. The private investigators can modify their locations more often, which critically reduces the possibility of detection by the target of the surveillance. This technique has been known for decades as the "ABC method." The ABC method refers to the three-person team of private investigators that are assigned to either the A, B, or C position in the surveillance activity. Investigator A stays behind the suspect, either on foot surveillance or behind the subject's vehicle, followed by B, the second investigator on foot or in a vehicle. The third investigator, C, remains on the opposite side of the street or on a parallel street if in a vehicle but always moves slightly ahead of or behind the subject of the surveillance. This allows for complete coverage of the target. It also allows the investigators to switch positions so that the same investigator is not behind the target for a long period of time. This reduces the chance that the target will identify any of the investigators and the surveillance that is being conducted against them. Although this method can cost the client more, there is a higher rate of success. With this type of surveillance, especially if using vehicles, secure two-way communication is vital.

### Undercover Surveillance

Undercover surveillance is one of the most interesting assignments for a private investigation. It is also the most difficult, time-consuming type of investigation and it can be very dangerous for the private investigator. This type of investigation is most often used in the workplace where the company will hire a private investigator to go undercover in the business to detect criminal activity, such as theft, drug smuggling operation in a business, fraud, or terrorism. It is imperative that the private investigator has a solid and plausible secret identity for this type of investigation. That identity is what the intelligence community calls a "legend." The secret identity is important because of the nature of undercover investigation; if the identity of the private investigator is discovered, the investigator could be in danger.

## Evidence

The private investigator often will find some evidence that could be used in a civil or criminal court proceeding related to an investigation. The private investigator must know how to collect and preserve evidence. The goal is identify the evidence, secure it, and establish a chain of custody. The private investigator will then be able to use such evidence and present it as admissible evidence in a court of law.

There are several steps related to the collection of evidence:

- Identify what the evidence is
- Secure the evidence
- Document the evidence with a photograph and/or a drawing
- Package the evidence in a proper manner
- Mark the evidence

- Preserve the evidence
- Establish a chain of custody of the evidence

All evidence collected by the private investigator may be used in a criminal or civil trial. The private investigator must guarantee that the evidence has been preserved and that the chain of custody for the evidence to be presented in court has not been interrupted or compromised in any manner whatsoever. To ensure this, the evidence must be properly identified and marked by the private investigator. The private investigator must show that the evidence is relevant to the case that is before the criminal or civil court.

## *Preemployment and Background Checks*

The private investigator may be contracted to conduct a preemployment or background investigation for a client. The preemployment investigation, as it states, is conducted on an applicant who is applying for a position. The background investigation can be requested for a variety of reasons. It may be an individual seeking to know more about a person they are dating, or to find out more information about the person before entering some business arrangement. It may be to inquire on individuals related to a criminal or civil matter for a law firm. The background investigation may also be related to criminal, espionage, or terrorism activities of a subject. Other than the fact that in a preemployment background investigation the private investigator will have a signed release from the application that allows the private investigator easy access to information on the applicant, the information that is investigated for both preemployment and background investigations, in most cases, will be the same based on the scope of the investigation.

The human resources department of organizations conducts initial screening and preemployment background investigations. Then they often utilize the service of a private investigator. This investigation process can be used to eliminate an applicant who may be predisposed to theft, industrial espionage, or even terrorism. A professional preemployment background investigation by a private investigator may determine if an individual is a possible future threat to the organization or homeland security based on their loyalty, lifestyle, or other issues that could lead to blackmail or need for money attained through espionage or any connection to a terrorist organization. A complete background investigation may expose an applicant who is attempting to obtain a position with the organization solely for the purpose of conducting industrial espionage, terrorism, or other criminal activity.

How in-depth the background investigation is conducted will depend on the applicant, position in the organization, position functions, and threat level. All of the following areas need to be examined for a full-scope background investigation. In some cases only some of the areas will be looked at or perhaps all but in not as much detail.

The applicant needs to complete a written application form in their own handwriting and it needs to be signed and dated by the applicant. Even if a resume was accepted online, at some point the written application needs to be completed. This will give the organization justification for not hiring the applicant or for termination should any false statements be discovered before or after hiring the applicant.

The areas that need to be investigated by the private investigator as part of the preemployment inquiry will include the following:

■ Criminal records
■ Civil records
■ Driving records
■ Employment history
■ Professional licenses and certifications
■ Education
■ Memberships
■ Financial history
■ Military service
■ Personal and professional references
■ Residence inquiry
■ Family
■ Lifestyle
■ Medical
■ Internet search history

## Criminal Records

A review of the applicant's criminal records by the private investigator is critical to reduce the threat of loss and industrial espionage. Depending on the jurisdiction in which the business is located, most local county courthouses and state governments allow a search of the criminal record. In some areas, this can be completed through the agency that has the records. In other situations, a criminal history record may need to be done in person at the local or state jurisdiction.

Private investigators will not be able to conduct government national criminal record checks. The only exception to this is if the organization is working with U.S. classified information as a contractor for the government. Even then, the company will not have access to a national criminal check, but the government investigating agency will.

Another area to search is the national sexual offender list. This is coordinated by the Department of Justice and enables every citizen to search the latest information from all 50 states, the District of Columbia, Puerto Rico, Guam, and numerous Indian tribes for the identity and location of known sex offenders. There are also such lists available on a state-by-state level that identifies convicted sexual offenders. An individual who is on a list and working for a company could be blackmailed to conduct criminal activity or could be a threat to employees and visitors.

Such lists also provide links so one can search registry websites maintained by individual jurisdictions. Note: The information contained in the national registry and the state and tribal registries is identical; the national registry simply enables a search across multiple jurisdictions.

## Civil Records

Civil records can be searched for records of divorce, marriage, or any civil action by or against the applicant. Special attention should be given to civil suits against the applicant or if the applicant has filed civil action against previous employers. This is especially important if any of the civil suits are against the individual for disclosure of company information or violation of any nondisclosure or noncompetitive agreements.

Civil records can also identify any property that an individual may own. This property could be a home, rental, or commercial business. The property could also be acreage with no structure on the land.

## Driving Records

When reviewing driving records from the state's department of motor vehicles, make note of the type of car the applicant owns and whether it fits with their current income level. Other areas that should be checked include any record of accidents, violations, suspension, or revocations of the applicant's driver's license. The driving records must also be checked for serious violations such as driving under the influence or any death by motor vehicle.

## Employment History

A review of the employment history should include all of the positions where the applicant has worked for at least the past 10 years. The details should encompass the title of their position, salary, duties, awards and achievements, supervisor's name, and the reason for leaving.

A red flag would include gaps in time, moving for a higher-level position and higher pay position to a position at a lower level and less pay. Periods of unemployment should be examined to determine why the applicant was unemployed.

If possible go to the employer in person. If that is not possible, then make contact by phone rather than by mail or e-mail in an attempt to verify employment and performance of the applicant.

## Professional Licenses and Certifications

If the position the applicant is applying for requires a professional license or certification, then verification of such credentials is a must. If there is no requirement for a special license or certification but the applicant lists some on the application, then they should be verified. Many individuals list items on applications to embellish their profile, thinking that the items listed will not be investigated. If the applicant lists false or unearned licenses or certifications, then this obliviously indicates that the person is dishonest and could be one who takes part in industrial espionage if the opportunity avails itself.

The types of licenses may vary from a commercial driver's license from the state, a pilot's license issued by the Federal Aviation Administration, a boat captain license from the U.S. Coast Guard, a medical license, or even a private investigator license issued by a state agency.

The certification may include teaching certifications from the state agency. Other certifications may be industry certifications, such as a Certified Protection Professional (CPP) from ASIS International, a Certified Safety Professional (CSP) from the American Society of Safety Engineers, or a Certified Confidentiality Officer (CCO) from the Business Espionage Controls and Countermeasures Association.

## Education

Educational credentials are important, especially if there are educational requirements for the position. The types of educational credentials may include

- High school diploma
- GED
- Trade school
- Two-year college
- Four-year university
- Graduate university
- Continuing college education

When documenting education at the high school or trade school level, a copy of the diploma should be provided. The private investigator should then call or write to the school for verification of the education. For college and university degrees, a copy of the diploma may be accepted but official school transcripts sent directly from the college or university to the employer is important. Ensure that the college or university is licensed by the state in which it is located. A reputable college or university will be accredited by one of the regional accrediting agencies in the United States as follows:

The Higher Learning Commission, Commission of the North Central Association of Colleges and Schools, 30 North LaSalle, Suite 2400, Chicago, IL 60602

Middle States Commission on Higher Education, 3624 Market Street, Philadelphia, PA 19104

New England Association of Schools and Colleges, Commission on Institutions of Higher Education, 209 Burlington Road, Bedford, MA 01730-1433

Northwest Commission on Colleges and Universities, 8060 165th Avenue, NW, Suite 100, Redmond, WA 98052; 425-558-4224

Southern Association of Schools and Colleges, Commission on Colleges, 1866 Southern Lane, Decatur, GA 30033-4097; 404-679-4500

Western Association of Schools and Colleges, Accrediting Commission for Senior Colleges and Universities, 985 Atlantic Avenue, Suite 100, Alameda, CA 94501; 510-748-9001

Western Association of Schools and Colleges, Accrediting Commission for Community and Junior Colleges, 10 Commercial Blvd., Suite 204, Novato, CA 94949; 415-506-0234

Degrees from colleges and universities that are unaccredited or unlicensed should not be accepted for the educational requirement for the applicant. Be aware of educational credentials from diploma mills. These are schools that are unlicensed and/or unaccredited and will issue illegitimate degrees for a fee.

## Memberships

Memberships listed by the applicant should be looked at very closely, as they can tell much about an individual, their interest and lifestyle. The memberships may include professional organizations related to the work of the applicant. Organizations may also include community or social groups. It is not permissible to ask the applicant about political or religious affiliations. Membership in any recognized subversive group is an issue of concern.

## Financial History

The financial history of the applicant is important to determine the individual's financial situation and any possible indebtedness and assets. Since the primary motive for industrial espionage is money, knowing the applicant's financial situation is critical in determining if there could be a threat of espionage, terrorism, or criminal activity. Investigating an applicant's financial history would include conducting a credit report and other financial reference searches with a signed release from the applicant.

## Military Service

The information that needs to be reviewed regarding an applicant's military service will include the branch of service. The federal branches of service are the Navy,

Army, Air Force, Marines, and Coast Guard. The applicant's dates of service, their duty assignments, any military training, awards, and any disciplinary action must be reviewed as part of the process.

The type of discharge, if no longer serving on active duty or in the Reserves, must be looked at closely. The accepted discharge should be honorable. A discharge for any other reason should be investigated to determine the reason of the separation. A review of the DD-214 and DD256N form issued by the military will confirm the type of discharge.

A search of military records can be done through the National Personnel Records Center, Military Personnel Records (NPRC-MPR), which is a repository of millions of military personnel, health, and medical records of discharged and deceased veterans of all services during the 20th century. (Records prior to WWI are in Washington, DC.) NPRC-MPR also stores medical treatment records of retirees from all branches of services, as well as records for dependent and other persons treated at Naval medical facilities. Information from these records is available upon written request (with signature and date) to the extent allowed by the law. The first step in the process is the completion of the Standard Form 180. It includes complete instructions for preparing and submitting requests. All requests must be in writing, signed, and mailed to the following address: National Personnel Records Center, 1 Archives Drive, St. Louis, MO 63138.

## Personal and Professional References

During the application process, personal and professional references are often requested. These references must be contacted. In most all cases, they will provide good references or the applicant would not have listed them. Ask the references if they know anyone who may also know the applicant. If the reference provides the organization with the name and contact information of additional individuals who know the applicant, then contact them and obtain an additional reference. This will provide more insight into the applicant's background.

## Residence Inquiries

When conducting a full background investigation, a residency inquiry by the private investigator may be conducted. The goal of this is to determine where the applicant has lived and to see if they were living within their reported means based on salary, their lifestyle, and to obtain references from landlords and neighbors.

Key areas to verify are the dates of residency, prompt payment of rent (if not a homeowner), the condition of the property, and why the applicant moved. Interaction with neighbors, evidence of criminal activity, positive community activity, and lifestyle can also be determined by a residence inquiry.

## Family

It is permissible to conduct an inquiry of the applicant's family if they will have access to company-protected information. Family members may present a conflict based on their position in life and in the workforce. Spouse and dependent children should be vetted to ensure that there are no threads from possible blackmail, national security issues, or foreign governments.

## Medical

The applicant's medical records can be reviewed with a signed release and only after a conditional offer of employment is made, according to the Americans with Disabilities Act. The company can also require a physical and psychological examination. The primary goal of the medical review is to ensure that the applicant is physically and mentally able to perform the duties of the position.

Any mental issues need to be explored to determine if the medical condition could lead to a situation where the individual may take part in industrial espionage and the compromise of company-protected information on their own or be easily convinced to do so.

## Internet and Social Media Search

A new focus of the background investigation is conducting an Internet and social media search of the applicant to see what links and photographs may be uncovered. Links such as Google, Facebook, LinkedIn, Twitter, and other social media should be explored. The applicant's name can also be run through various search links to see if something appears.

## Periodic and Promotional Update Investigations

After an applicant is hired, a private investigator may be used to conduct a periodic or promotional investigation. This occurs if the person has had access to protected information and there is some concern that the employee may be involved in criminal activity, espionage, or terrorism. It can also be a routine periodic investigation as a preventive measure for individuals with access to protected information.

All individuals with access to company-protected information should have an updated background investigation every 5 years. This is an excellent tool in preventing espionage, terrorism, and theft, and a service the private investigator can provide to the client and in protection of the homeland.

An updated investigation should also be conducted when a current employee is being promoted or their duties changed where they will now have access to company-protected information that they have not had access to in the past.

## Use of Nondisclosure and Noncompete Agreements

Nondisclosure agreements are utilized to protect organizations from unauthorized disclosure of protected and confidential company information from current or former employees, and provide for a civil penalty for such disclosure either during employment or after leaving employment with the organization. There could still be criminal action if the information released was stolen and considered espionage. The organization's legal staff should develop a nondisclosure agreement form to meet the specific needs of the organization. A private investigator may be hired to confirm if the employee or former employee violated such an agreement.

Likewise, a noncompete agreement is used to prevent a former employee for taking their knowledge from the company they are leaving to a competitor. Various samples and templates can be found online and modified to suit a specific business's needs. As it is related to espionage, it can prevent an employee from revealing confidential and protected information and allow for civil recourse if the agreement is violated.

A private investigator may be hired to investigate a current or former employee to determine if there has been a violation of these agreements. Confirmation of such violations could lead to civil action against the current or former employee and may require court testimony from the private investigator.

## Counterespionage and Fraud

"Espionage is not a game; it's a struggle we must win if we are to protect our freedom and our way of life." These words, spoken by President Ronald Reagan during a November 30, 1985, radio speech, have never been more relevant (Figure 5.1).

A private investigator is often hired to investigate possible industrial espionage of company confidential information and fraud activities within an organization. In order to conduct a counterespionage and fraud investigation, the private investigator must have an understanding of what espionage is, as well as the threat to business, and homeland and national security. The private investigator must also have an understanding of the methods of espionage and fraud. This is a vital role for the private investigator as it relates to homeland security.

Espionage is the gathering of information by intelligence agents or terrorists as a strategy for gaining superiority over enemies. Intelligence officers are those individuals working for government intelligence services who are trained to serve their country by gathering information. Spies betray their country and/or their employer by committing espionage.

### Methods of Espionage

Industrial espionage is frequently conducted by using fundamental business intelligence-gathering methods. The Internet and dozens of commercial databases

**Figure 5.1    President Ronald Reagan. (Photograph by Daniel J. Benny.)**

are generally available, along with such sources such as trade journals and company newsletters and annual reports.

Many countries conduct espionage by sending their representatives to the United States on fact-finding visits or for training to obtain information. Cultural and military exchanges, visitor programs, trade shows, participants in scientific meetings, and other such methods are used. Another method is to send scholars—and students, in some cases—to obtain positions at universities and educational institutions, particularly those that conduct research for the government, to accumulate information and data.

## Counterespionage and Fraud Audits

As part of the counterespionage and fraud investigation, the private investigator may be hired to conduct counterespionage and fraud audits. The goal of the audits is to determine if all of the policies, procedures, and physical security measures related to the safeguarding of protected and classified information are being adhered to. As 1960s loss prevention consultant Sal Astor stated in his Astor's Laws of Loss Prevention, a loss prevention program will only fail upon audit. In other words, if an organization conducts no audits on the counterespionage program, the organization will not know that there is a problem or failure in the system until a loss occurs and such loss is discovered. With no audits, there is the assumption that all is fine, but that is of course a false sense of security. Once protected information has been compromised, is not the time that an organization should become aware of such a loss.

All areas related to the counterespionage program should be audited on a regular basis as well as on the use of surprise audits. This would include audits on the protected information in which inventory is examined to ensure that all information is accounted for. The audit should include an inspection of the documents and information to ensure that they are properly marked, kept in secure storage, and access to security containers or computer systems that contain documents and protected information are restricted and documented.

The list of cleared company employees who have access must also be reviewed during the audit to ensure that those individuals are still authorized and have access only to information on a need-to-know basis. In addition, documentation regarding employee security awareness training should be verified during the audit process.

Computer system passwords and security container combinations need to be memorized and not written down. During the audits, attention needs to be given to computer passwords or security container combinations that may have been written down in areas that could be located by an individual with intent on committing industrial espionage.

### Counterespionage and Fraud Investigations

Counterespionage and fraud investigations by the private investigator may be started at any point in time when there is a violation of security policy. This type of investigation may also be based on a report of adverse information or indications that industrial espionage is taking place.

Security violations may be identified during the counterespionage audit or it may be reported to security. All violations need to be adequately investigated in order to identify the violation and who was involved. The investigation should be used to correct the situation and remove the risk of industrial espionage.

If the organization is operating under the National Industrial Security Program Operating Manual (NISPOM), that procedure requires that cleared defense contractor employees report to their respective security department any adverse information regarding other cleared employees. This may include excessive indebtedness and financial problems, unexplained affluence, use of drugs or excessive use of intoxicants, unusual behavior, mental or emotional problems, and criminal activity and convictions.

## Counterterrorism

The private investigator may be hired to conduct a counterterror investigation for an organization. This can include the investigation of activity by employees of the company that could have ties to terrorism. It may also be an investigation to determine if a company is being targeted by a terrorist group. To understand and counter the threat from terrorism, it is important that the private investigator have a grasp of the strategies and tactics employed by terrorist organizations. It is also important to understand why they are such a threat.

## Terrorism

You may have heard the words, "One man's terrorist is another man's freedom fighter." It may be hard to agree on what a freedom fighter is, but a group of individuals who specifically target civilians are not freedom fighters, they are terrorists. A dead terrorist is a good terrorist.

There are many different definitions of terrorism. The most direct definition is the use or threat of violence to obtain specific goals. What are the goals of terrorist organizations? There are four:

*Political goals*—A political goal is to change the leadership or political structure of a country. For example, the conflict between the United Kingdom and Ireland over the control of Northern Ireland. Although both sides often had different religious affiliations, the real issue was political.

*Ideological goals*—This includes terrorist groups whose goal is to stop a certain practice. This can also include animal rights, environmental, or antiabortion groups who take part in criminal acts in support of their ideological cause.

*Religious goals*—Some terrorist organizations base their actions on religious views, such as Islamic Jihadists. Their goal is to convert the earth to Islam, by force if necessary. Islamic Jihadist goals, including those of ISIS, are also political and ideological because Islam is a way of life and is their political and judicial system.

*Violence for effect*—Their ultimate goal is to influence an audience beyond the immediate victim(s). They want to attract attention to their cause, demonstrate power, exact revenge, obtain logistical support to carry out terrorist operations, and, if possible, cause government overreaction to gain support of the masses and media.

## Terrorist Categories

There are three specific categories of terrorists: state directed, state supported, and non-state supported. State directed is when a country uses terrorism as a matter of their national policy, such as Iran. State supported is when a country provides aid to terrorism in the form of money, weapons, or harboring terrorists in their country, as was the case with Iraq. Non-state supported are terrorist groups that operate independently with no assistance from a nation. This could include domestic groups such as the Ku Klux Klan or Black Panthers.

There are two broad categories of terrorist organizations. National terrorists operate within the boundaries of a single nation in order to affect issues related to that nation. Transnational terrorists operate in a region or worldwide to affect issues that impact numerous nations and regions or have global impact.

## Typical Profile of a Terrorist

While a terrorist can be anyone, there are some typical profiles that have emerged over the years. Generally, terrorists have been male, between the ages of 22 and 28, unmarried, of urban origin, and have a university-level education. They are often upper middle class in their society and are often recruited from universities, religious groups, and prisons.

Most foreign terrorists to the United States are Marxist or Islamic Jihadist. Most domestic terrorists in the United States are anti-government, Marxist, Islamic Jihadist, or racist groups.

## Use of Criminal Profiling for Counterterrorism

Criminal profiling is not new to law enforcement, intelligence, and security agencies, and are a part of the investigative and intelligence process. It has been utilized in efforts to identify and apprehend individuals involved in various types of criminal activity, including serial murders, organized crime, drug cartels and crimes related to illegal drugs, espionage, hate groups, and terrorist organizations.

When utilizing criminal profiling as an investigative tool, it is vital that law enforcement, intelligence, and security agencies base it on the facts of the case and not on bias or stereotyping. It needs to be based on objective data with numerous descriptive variables so that the range of offenders can be narrowed.

It is important that law enforcement, intelligence, and security agencies not be restricted in performing their duties in identifying a suspect in terrorism because of political correctness. Criminal profiling is an accepted tool and should never be disregarded because of political correctness or because someone is offended.

Racial profiling is often confused with criminal profiling and in the minds of some it is one and the same. Racial profiling can be defined as investigating an individual or taking a law enforcement or security action against an individual based on race, national origin, religion, ethnicity, or sexual orientation. Oftentimes what some might say is racial profiling is nothing more than the perception that it is occurring, when in fact it was a clear case of the proper use of criminal profiling. In any event, some might say perceptions are everything. In the matter of offended feelings and misguided perceptions, they are not a justifiable reason to prohibit the law enforcement, intelligence, and security community from performing their duties effectively in providing protection from terrorism through criminal profiling.

In order to counter terrorism, criminal profiling can be a viable tool when properly utilized.

## Organizational Structure of Terrorist Groups

Though each terrorist group could be organized differently, there are some common structures. Hardcore leadership is the management of the organization. It may include individuals or groups of individuals who control a particular terrorist organization.

The active cadre is the individuals in a terrorist organization who carry out the terrorist acts and collect intelligence for target selection. They will also be involved in gathering logistics support in the field such as vehicles, weapons, and safe houses. The structure of the active cadre is that of small cells made up of four to six individuals. This is done for security reasons. The cells are organized by function, such as the intelligence cell that conducts intelligence missions for target selection. There are the logistics cells that secure weapons, explosives, vehicles, and safe houses. The tactical cell carries out the terrorist activity.

Active supporters are individuals who provide behind-the-scenes support for the terrorist organization. The support may include legal support, laundering of money, medical support, or political support. Passive supporters are the useful idiot. They donate money, conduct fundraising, or take part in public demonstrations in support of their cause.

## Operational Tactics

The operational tactics is how the terrorism is carried out or method of operation. The most common tactic is the use of explosives. This allows the group to make a simple or complex explosive based on the funds and capabilities of the group members. There are numerous methods of activating an explosive device such as a timer, altimeter, light sensor, radio frequencies, pressure or trip wire, and suicide bombing. This allows the terrorist to escape capture or to die for their cause as a suicide bomber.

Assassinations are used to take out a specific target. The target may be a political leader, law enforcement member, or any selected person. Hijacking an aircraft or other mode of transportation or taking a group hostage are other tactics. Kidnapping, armed assault, robberies, burglaries, and fraud are used to obtain money or weapons. Street action is used to infiltrate demonstrations and cause unrest. The most effective tactic is the element of surprise.

## Target Selection

Target selection involves picking and identifying an individual, group of individuals, or a structure to strike. The terrorist group seeks a target that is soft, visible, and has high-impact value. A soft target is one that does not have a high level of security. General aviation airports or aircraft are considered soft targets as well as concerts and restaurants, as was seen in the 2015 Paris terrorist attacks. A visible target is one that is well known, such as the World Trade Center or a national monument. A high impact target is one that will cause much damage or loss of life and will obtain the most media attention.

## U.S. Domestic Terrorist Threats

There are a variety of domestic threats within the United States. Such groups may be politically left wing or right wing. The agenda of these groups may be antigovernment, environmental, animal rights, antiabortion, religious, or racists.

## U.S. Foreign Terrorist Threats

There are many international terror organizations, but the most dangerous to the United States are the Islamic Jihadist groups. They are such a serious threat because, since Islam is founded on the teachings of the Prophet Muhammad, it is their religion and they will die for it. It allows them the ability to unite followers through militant Islam. Radical Islamic terrorists in the United States are the most serious threat as is evident based on the 9/11, Fort Hood, Boston Marathon, and the two-person ISIS cell in San Bernardino, California, attacks.

The goal of the Islamic Jihadist is to reform and convert the earth by force if necessary. As many as 18 to 29 percent of the followers of Islam are Jihadist, which equates to 2,230,000 Jihadist followers in the United States alone. They have a network of over 160 Hezbollah organizations worldwide of experienced forces. Money is no object to support the cause and they have transnational capabilities.

## Counterterrorism Methods

Organizations must be proactive to counter the threat of terrorism. As part of the risk and threat analysis, the private investigator must examine the possible threat from terrorism and must calculate that information into the security equation.

Intelligence is key in assessing the threat from terrorism and developing counterterrorism measures. Sources of intelligence the private investigator can access for their client would include the news and current events, liaison with local law enforcement agencies, the Department of Homeland Security, and security consultants.

## Signs of Terrorism

To counter terrorism, it is important to be alert to what is occurring at or around the target location. There are some distinctive signs of possible terrorist activity against a business that the private investigator should investigate and provide awareness training to their client. The following are the common signs identified by the Department of Homeland Security. Some or all of these signs could be observed near a target location or near an individual if they become a target of terrorism.

- Surveillance
- Elicitation
- Tests of security
- Acquiring supplies
- Suspicious people who do not belong
- Dry runs
- Deploying assets/getting into position

## Surveillance

When terrorists have chosen a specific target, that area will be observed during the planning phase of the operation to gather intelligence. The goal is to determine the strengths, weaknesses, and number of personnel that may respond to an incident. Routes to and from the target are established during the surveillance phase. It is important to take note of suspicious activity.

## Elicitation

The second sign is elicitation. This is when an individual is attempting to gain information about the organization, person, or operations of the site. An example is someone attempting to gain knowledge about the type of activity, security, or hours of staffing. By obtaining part-time or full-time positions on the property, information can be obtained in that manner as well.

## Tests of Security

Tests of security is another area in which terrorists could attempt to gather information and intelligence about the target location. They may set off alarms and document the response. They may attempt to enter a structure or facility on a pretext to observe the level of security. They could leave an empty bag that an explosive could be placed in, near the target to see if anyone notices and responds to the bag or container as a test of security alertness and response procedures.

## Acquiring Supplies

Acquiring supplies is the activity when the terrorists begin to obtain what they will need to aid in the success of their terror operation. It may include stealing security or police uniforms or company uniforms to allow easy access to a target site. It might be to obtain weapons, explosives, vehicles, or safe house to use in the operation. It can be whatever the terrorist cell needs for that operation to be carried out in an effective and successful manner.

## Dry Runs

At the dry run stage the terrorists are making their final test before the actual terror strike. They will now simulate the attack in complete detail to make sure that they have the operations procedure down and that the attack will be successful as planned.

## Deploying Assets/Getting into Position

The final sign is when the terrorists are deploying assets or getting into position. This is perhaps the last opportunity that security will have to take action and alert authorities before the terrorist act takes place. It is also important to note that such preincident indicators and activity might occur months or even years apart. It is extremely important to be alert and report all information received no matter how trifle it may appear. That information needs to be forwarded to local police and the Department of Homeland Security.

# The Internet and Cybersecurity

## Using the Internet and Social Media for Private Investigations

In a recent nationwide survey conducted by PoliceOne and LexisNexis, state, federal, and local law enforcement professionals stated that they used social media as part of their investigative methods. The utilization of the Internet and social media by the private investigator in conducting an investigation is also occurring. It is a useful tool that should not be overlooked by the private investigator in order to protect businesses and the homeland.

Private investigators will continue to use traditional methods of surveillance and investigation, but the use of social media and the Internet can provide valuable information and facts on individuals and organizations. Before a private investigator goes out on a case to a surveillance location, the private investigator can use the computer to observe aerial photographs as well as streetview photographs of the surveillance location in order to plan the assignment. This is a valued planning tool for the private investigator and can allow the private investigator to be prepared before going out on assignment.

Private investigators can also explore sites such as Facebook and Twitter to obtain valuable information that may aid in their investigation. The use of social media provides private investigators the ability to confirm what they may already suspect and enables them to follow leads that may allow them to acquire more information on the case. Private investigators can capitalize on their success by monitoring these social media sites when investigating possible terrorist activity. Terror groups such as ISIS use social media to recruit and communicate all over the globe.

The use of the Internet for investigations by the private investigator aids in vetting potential employees and potential business associates for an organization. This investigative process is also helpful when conducting background and pre-employment investigations for a client. The searches that the private investigator can utilize on the Internet when conducting investigations may include the following:

- Deep Internet research
- Social media search using Web 2.0
- Review of blogs
- Public records
- Blogs
- Social media
- E-mail addresses
- Online profiles
- Company web pages

## *Cybersecurity Defined*

With the global use of the Internet, an entire new area for cybersecurity concerns has been created. In order for private investigators to operate in this environment, they must know how to protect their own assets and those of clients they will be working with. For private investigators who specialize in cybersecurity prevention and investigation, this knowledge is even more critical. It is also vital to have an understanding as to what the Internet is.

The Internet is an open, global network supporting standard utilities such as e-mail, file transfer, social media, news groups, and the World Wide Web. The World Wide Web is a set of graphical, hyperlinked applications accessible over an organization's Internet. The Internet has opened a global communications medium that is used for internal communications, customer service and support, sales and distribution, electronic banking, marketing and research, and the storage of company confidential information as well as government classified information (Figure 5.2).

There are several types of websites. The interactive site can be customized for the user and is primarily utilized for one-to-one communications. The transaction site allows account inquiry and online transactions. Publishing websites provide reports, statistics, and other types of publications for marketing. The site is an online brochure or sales vehicle for an organization.

**Figure 5.2  Personal computers must be considered with regard to Internet security and cybersecurity prevention. (Photograph by Daniel J. Benny.)**

Protection of the Internet and company and government information is the end-system user's responsibility. The threat to your system and information can come from hackers, competitors, governments, customers or clients, contractors, or employees. They can wreak havoc on the Internet through the destruction or modification of your data as will be discussed in this chapter.

Most states have laws relating to computer crime, and it is also a federal offense and falls under Title 18, Section 1030 and Title 18, Section 2701. The Federal Bureau of Investigation has primary jurisdiction over all traditional investigations related to national defense, foreign relations, or any restricted data that can be used to cause damage to the United States. The U.S. Secret Service has primary jurisdiction over criminal acts involving consumer reporting or U.S. Treasury computers. The Federal Bureau of Investigation and Secret Service have concurrent jurisdiction over financial institution fraud.

## The Threat from Cybersecurity

### Adware

Adware is software that displays an advertisement on the target computer by use of a pop-up. If clicked on, the adware may install itself on the computer, slowing the computer, and can hijack the browser. The adware may also retrieve information from a computer or computer network, which can be used for industrial espionage.

## Anonymizing Proxies

If an employee or asset wants to hide their web browsing on a company computer, anonymizing proxies is the process that is utilized. It also allows the user to bypass security filters that have been put in place.

## Autorun Worm

Autorun worm malicious programs are able to access the computer through the Window AutoRun feature on the target computer. They most often can invade the computer with the introduction of a USB device to spread the autorun worm.

## Chain Letter or E-Mail Malware

Chain letter or e-mail malware comes in the form of an e-mail letter that attempts to encourage the user to open the e-mail and forward the email to other individuals. By clicking on the link, it will allow a virus or Trojan into the computer. It may also be used to spread rumors and false information harmful to the organization or send out e-mails under the company's name.

## Cookies

A cookie is a file that is inserted onto the computer to allow the website to remember information on the user. This in itself is not a security issue. The concern is that it can also be used to track the browsing history of the user for commercial marketing, but more important to obtain information for possible industrial espionage or a terrorist attack.

## Data Theft, Leakage, and Loss

The unauthorized transfer of data and information from an organization's computer is called data theft, leak, or loss. This is one of the most common methods used for industrial espionage or to obtain information on an organization that is the target of terrorism.

## Denial of Service

A denial-of-service attack on an organization's computer network prevents an authorized user from accessing websites and information on a company computer. This can be used to sabotage and disrupt the organization's computer system.

## Domain Name System Hijacking

In domain name system hijacking, the attacker changes the domain name setting so that it is ignored or controlled by another domain name. This allows access to the computer and information for industrial espionage.

## Fraudulent Antivirus Malware

Fraudulent antivirus malware alerts the computer user to a nonexistent virus in the computer, so that they click on the link provided. This will then allow a real virus into the computer that can be used to obtain protected information.

## Internet Worms

This is a virus that when opened will reproduce itself across the local computer network and even on the Internet. It may infect computers beyond those of the target company.

## Keylogger

A keylogger is a device that is plugged into the computer and will record all keystrokes. A keylogger is used by an individual wishing to take part in industrial espionage. A keylogger will give the hacker the ability to identify the passwords on the computer. They will then be able to come back at a later time and log into the computer using the stolen passwords undetected. Use of the password will then make it appear that any information taken was done so by the person whose password was stolen.

## Mobile Phone Malware

Mobile phone malware is designed to run on a mobile and/or smart phone in order to retrieve all of the information stored in the phone. This could include calls made, phone numbers, text messages, photographs, and apps that have been accessed.

## Phishing

Phishing is the process of sending out fraudulent e-mail representing a legitimate organization such as a bank or credit card company in an attempt to induce the target to provide sensitive information. This will allow the perpetrator to access accounts, computers, and other sources of information.

## Social Networking Threats

With the use of social networking, there is the threat of industrial espionage. It may be from providing too much open source information on sites such as Facebook. Information can also be obtained on social sites by the use of pretext attempts to obtain the information.

## Spyware

Spyware once installed on the computer allows those taking part in espionage to retrieve information from the computer or computer network.

## Trojan

The Trojan can be a serious threat. It can enter the computer by disguising itself as a known software. Once downloaded on the computer, it will add itself to the computer start-up process. It can monitor everything on the computer and even generate e-mail from the infected computer.

## Countering Cybersecurity Attacks

As in developing a traditional loss prevention program, the private investigator can conduct a risk assessment based on the projected use of the Internet and company computers and possible risk. Computer security procedures need to be based on the greatest risk. The computer security program to prevent industrial espionage has a least two levels of protection for the most sensitive information, and treats the infrastructure and applications as two distinct but mutually dependent areas. In keeping with Astor's Fifth Law of Loss Prevention, "any loss prevention control fails only upon audit." Ensure that there are strict monitoring and reporting procedures to support your security policy. Issues to consider are what services are allowed, what services or sites will be blocked, what is considered acceptable usage, the usage habits of employees, e-mail, and how the security policy will be enforced.

As part of the protection plan, minimize the number of connections to the Internet and control them. Increase the security of each connected computer and strengthen the network perimeter. The goal is to keep outsiders out but allow insiders access to perform their assigned duties.

The key factors in the protection of assets through the Internet are the development of a sound security policy and the use of proxy firewalls when possible. Ensure that the firewall software is up to date and examine the security of modem connections to avoid end-runs.

Conduct inspections and penetration testing software against your system. By following these guidelines an organization can reduce the threat of loss through the Internet.

The following are specific steps that can be taken to prevent the loss of protected information from espionage attacks against company computers and computer networks.

*Anti-malware*—This is software that can protect information on the organization's computer from viruses, malware, worms, and Trojans. The anti-malware product scans the computer to identify programs that are not authorized. Once the malware is identified, it can be destroyed, eliminating the threat.

*Anti-spam*—This software can identify unwanted e-mails from reaching the inbox of the organization's computer. Most important is that many of these types of e-mails may be used to introduce viruses and malware into the system when opened. They can be used to obtain protected information. Not only are annoying e-mails stopped, but the potential for industrial espionage is reduced as well.

*Application control*—This is the process of blocking the use of identified applications that could compromise the security of the company Internet system and information by the use of firewalls. This will not only prevent the loss of information but can be used to prevent staff from operating unauthorized applications on the company Internet system.

*Encryption*—Encryption is the coding of information sent, received, and stored to prevent unauthorized access and theft of sensitive information. The only way the encryption can be read is by an authorized individual with the capability of decoding the encrypted information.

*Firewall*—A firewall is a barrier between computer networks to prevent malicious traffic that could be used to damage or retrieve information from obtaining access. In addition to preventing access, a firewall can identify the threat and provide warning that an attempt was made and has been blocked.

*Intrusion prevention system*—This is a system that monitors all activity on the company computer and provides notification of threats or problems. It is not only a preventative tool but also an investigative tool to aid in the identification from whom the attack might have originated.

*Network access control*—This includes the authorization of those employees who are authorized to enter the system. It also includes the assessment of those trying to enter the system and the enforcement of company security policies.

*URL content filtering*—This is utilized to block categories or specific websites that the organization does not want staff accessing from company computers. This not only prevents staff from browsing non-work-related websites, but stops viruses that may be introduced into the computer network when unauthorized websites are opened.

## Report Writing

One of the most important aspects of the private investigator's investigation is to document the investigation in a written report. The private investigator needs to ensure that all notes and observations are documented as soon as possible in the written report. The private investigator will use the written report to provide the client with the results of the investigation conducted for the client. An investigative report should be considered a legal document, as it could be subpoenaed under discovery for a civil or criminal court proceeding. The report needs to represent all relevant aspects of the investigation. An investigative report needs to be accurate, objective, understandable, organized, and timely. The private investigator's report must contain the detailed facts of the case and be presented in a professional manner.

Investigative reports should be typed with justified margins and the pages numbered in a manner such as "Page 1 of 5." The investigative report should include the following parts:

- Introduction—Describes the scope of the investigation.
- Summary—This is an overview of the private investigator's investigation.
- Conclusion—The final results of the investigation and in what way did it help the client relate to the service provided.
- Closing—Thank the customer for hiring the investigator and advise of one's availability for additional investigative work.
- Exhibits—Any evidence such as photographs and records should be attached as exhibits.

The investigative report is a legal document and could be requested under discovery related to criminal or civil action for up to 7 years. It is vital that the private investigator keeps copies of all reports for at least 7 years. The investigative report is also the professional product of the private investigator. In the end not only the information provided but how it is provided in a professional investigative report is a representation of the private investigator and their professional image.

## Court Testimony

The private investigator will often be called upon to present court testimony with regard to an investigation they have conducted. The best investigation can be rendered ineffective if the private investigator cannot communicate the facts to those who must understand and believe in them. This is particularly true in the daunting atmosphere of a courtroom. By understanding the role of the testimony in the court proceedings and knowing how to provide testimony effectively, the private investigator can be successful in the courtroom.

## *Testimony*

Testimony is the means by which the fact finder, be it judge or jury, learns about the relevant facts from the private investigator. Testimony is the means by which the private investigator will convey what they know to those who do not know but should. The subject of testimony of the private investigator will include what the investigator did during the investigation and the facts of the case that were established.

The three goals of testifying are to be understood, be believed, and be remembered in a positive manner. Being understood means to speak clearly and understand the question before you start to answer. Speak English and not investigative slang and jargon. The private investigator needs to be a witness, not a lawyer.

No case is worth the private investigator's personal honesty. One lie in court or out will prevent the investigator from being an effective private investigator ever again. By telling the truth one does not need to remember what to say. Be consistent. Variations in testimony will be exploited by the defense. Be candid and understand that no case is perfect; if it were, it wouldn't be in court. Always be fair. Treat all parties with respect, whether they deserve it or not. Unfairness makes the private investigator the bad guy in the minds of the jury. Be thorough, as too many loose ends and assumptions in the investigation make the private investigator look sloppy and uncaring, and therefore unbelievable. Prepare for court. If the private investigator does not care enough, no one else will either. Reread reports or notes, but do not memorize them. Stay within your qualifications and knowledge.

Being remembered is important. Some private investigators have a natural flair, but that is not the only way to be memorable. The private investigator needs to be sure they are memorable in a positive way. A professional appearance and a professional attitude go a long way. Good manners are invaluable in court. Body language will reinforce or distract from the testimony. The private investigator needs to be aware of himself. Jurors remember best what they see and hear first and last. First impressions are important, as are last impressions. Physical exhibits collected by the private investigator also make the investigator memorable. People remember what they see more than what they hear.

Credibility is also a vital aspect of the private investigator's court testimony. The fact finder should be told about the investigator's education, training, and experience. The investigator needs to be prepared to explain where they obtained their expertise in the specific area making the investigator appease the "expert." Credentials convey that the private investigator is well versed in the area of the case they investigated.

An investigator should recognize the difference between different court proceedings. A preliminary hearing, for the defense, is to discover the private investigator's case, its strength and weaknesses, and to get details on record for later use. Counsel will be friendlier and inquisitive. Pretrial hearings may test probable cause or propriety of an officer's actions. Details of why the private investigator did things will be important. Trial is the place the Trojan horse will be opened, and you will be attacked.

## Tactics of the Defense

The duty of the defense attorney consists of furthering the best interest of the defendant, which usually means beating the case. The goal therefore is to make the testimony of the private investigator less understandable, less believable, and less memorable. The defense attorney or district attorney may try to change the private investigator's psychological frame of reference, even before they take the stand. The defense attorney or district attorney is not the private investigator's friend. They are always on the other side. The investigator should never forget that concept.

## Techniques of the Defense

- Condescending
- Unintelligence
- Overly friendly or overly aggressive
- Demanding yes or no answers
- Reversing or revising the investigator's name or words
- Suggesting conflicts in answers
- Repeating questions
- Trying to confuse the private investigator

## General Statements about Testifying

- Be professional.
- If required it is permissible to explain an answer. Ask the judge for permission.
- Never argue with counsel.
- Never apologize for doing your job.
- Be aware of body language.
- There is a saying, source unknown, that one witness doesn't win a case alone, but one witness can lose a case alone. Don't let it be you.

# Bibliography

Association of Certified Fraud Examiners. *Corporate Espionage*. Austin, TX: Association of Certified Fraud Examiners, 2016.

Federal Bureau of Investigation. Sex offender registry websites. 2013. http://www.fbi.gov /scams-safety/registry.

Fischer, R. J. and G. Green. *Introduction to Security*. Burlington, MA: Elsevier, 2012.

National Archives. Military personnel records. 2013. http://www.archives.gov/st-louis/military -personnel/.

National Counterintelligence Center. *Annual Report to Congress on Foreign Economic Collection and Industrial Espionage*. Washington, DC: U.S. Government Printing Office, 2011.

## Chapter 6

# Other Private Investigation Services Related to Homeland Security

Private investigators who have experience in specialized investigative-related areas can provide additional services to clients. The ability of a private investigator to provide services such as security consulting, expert witness testimony, technical surveillance countermeasures, protective services, investigative photography, and process services will be of value to the investigator to increase his work and profits, be of more value to clients, and in protecting the homeland.

## Security Consulting

Private investigators with experience in specialized areas of security such as physical security, network security, protective service, cultural proper security, maritime security, and aviation security can provide security consultation and training to clients.

One of the primary areas of security consulting as it relates to homeland security is the use of physical security and protective systems. Physical security measures need to be utilized as part of a comprehensive security program. Physical security will aid in the protection of life, sensitive information, property, as well as facility structures.

**Note:** This chapter will provide a generic overview of the components of a physical security program. The physical measures described can be used in various areas of security. The physical security sensors described are both current and older technology. Older security sensors and systems are discussed, as they may still be found at some locations and can still be utilized as part of a total security system. If there are upgrades in the system or there is new construction, the most current technology and security sensors and systems should be utilized.

The goals of physical security are to

*Deter entry*—The use of signs, intrusion detection systems, barriers, locks, access control, metal detectors, x-ray, and security cameras can deter individuals from taking part in criminal and terror activity.

*Delay entry*—By utilizing various physical security measures, should an individual not be deterred and attempt to take part in criminal activity, the physical security measures put in place can delay the perpetrator. During this period of delay, the perpetrator may be observed by a security officer, staff, or local law enforcement, and the crime can be averted.

*Detect entry*—With the use of physical security devices, should an individual attempt to take part in criminal activity, their presence and actions will be detected. This could result in the perpetrator stopping the criminal activity. It could result in the detection by security officers or staff, and apprehension by law enforcement. If a crime or loss of property is detected, management knows that there has been a threat and they can evaluate the adequacy of the current physical security system to prevent future threats.

Physical security measures can help control movement throughout a facility: movement of vehicles, people (including visitors and employees), as well as controlling access of individuals arriving or leaving a facility, and securing any restricted areas throughout a facility.

## Intrusion Detection Systems

An intrusion detection system is designed to provide notice of someone entering a protected area. This is accomplished by a system of sensors that sends a notification to the computer base's monitoring stations or to a local sound-producing device when the sensor is activated. The intrusion detection system can be a proprietary central station in which the system is monitored by the owner within its property. It can also be a contract central station. The contract central station is a contract security monitoring service not located or associated with the property being protected. The contract central station receives the alarm and then notifies perhaps police, fire, emergency medical services, local law enforcement, or the organization's security department or management on the type of alarm that is received.

The most common sensors that are utilized include:

*Electromagnetic contacts*—They are used to provide protection for doors and windows. Contacts are placed on the door and doorframe or the window and window sash. When the door or window is closed the contacts match together. When the alarm system is activated, a current passes through the matching contacts. When the door or window is opened while the alarm is activated, it breaks the circuit and the alarm is activated (Figure 6.1).

*Photoelectric sensor*—This sensor is utilized to provide protection of doors and passageways or entrances to a sensitive area based on the use of a light beam. When an individual breaks the light beam, the alarm is activated. While ties are not used any longer, they may be found in old security systems. The photoelectric cell can also be used to automatically activate security lighting during periods of darkness.

*Laser*—This sensor can provide protection of doors and passageways, and is based on the use of a laser light beam. When the laser beam is broken, the alarm is activated. It can also be used to automatically activate security lighting during periods of darkness.

*Glass breakage*—This sensor is used on glass windows or door areas with glass to detect attempted entry through the breaking of glass. The sensor is mounted on the glass itself or near the glass window or door glass area, and detects the vibration of the breaking glass.

*Pressure*—This sensor is used to detect a person walking on a surface on the interior of a structure or the exterior grounds. The pressure-sensitive sensor is placed under the carpet inside a property. If used outdoors, it is buried under the surface of the ground when used. The alarm is activated when an individual walks over the surface where the sensor is concealed.

**Figure 6.1   Electromagnetic sensor. (Photograph by Daniel J. Benny.)**

*Vibration*—This is used to provide protection in utility ports large enough for an individual to access. When a perpetrator attempts to access an area protected by this sensor and touches the vibration sensor, it will activate the alarm.

*Audio*—This sensor is a microphone and in most cases a series of microphones that are placed inside the facility to be protected. Should there be an unauthorized access into the structure, the microphones are activated. The microphones can transmit all that is heard to a central station monitored by the property security department or at a contract central station. The security officer can then dispatch a response and notify the local police.

*Ultrasonic*—This sensor is used for interior protection of a facility when not occupied. The sensor transceiver sends out sonar waves across the room that transverse back to the transceiver in a timed sequence. Should a perpetrator enter the protected area, the sonar waves are interrupted and the alarm is activated. It is not recommended for hangars, because the air movement that can occur can set off the alarm.

*Microwave*—This sensor transceiver is used for interior protection of a facility when not occupied. The sensor transceiver sends out microwaves across the room that transverses back to the transceiver in a timed sequence. Should a perpetrator enter the protected area, the microwaves are interrupted and the alarm is activated. This sensor should not be used in a room with large areas of glass, as it will penetrate the glass and could result in false alarms. It may also be used to protect outdoor areas with restricted access (Figure 6.2).

*Passive infrared*—This sensor is the best motion transceiver for use in interior protection of an unoccupied facility (Figure 6.3). The sensor transceiver sends

**Figure 6.2  Microwave sensor on the White House lawn. (Photograph by Daniel J. Benny.)**

**Figure 6.3 Passive infrared. (Photograph by Daniel J. Benny.)**

out light energy that detects body heat. Should a perpetrator enter the protected area, the passive infrared detects the heat of the person, and the heat in the protected area and the alarm is activated. This sensor is recommended.

*Capacitance proximity*—This sensor is used to protect metal safes and metal security containers. Once the sensor is attached to the metal safe or metal security container, a magnetic field around the protected item is established. The magnetic field will extend one foot around the protected safe or container. When a person walks into that space or touches the safe or container, their body will draw in the magnetism. This will cause a drop in the magnetic field protecting the safe or security container and activate the alarm. This could be used for a safe or key security container.

*Sonar*—Sonar can be used to protect water access to a facility such as a lake, river, or sea. By placing a sonar sensor in the waters near the facility, it can provide early warning of an intrusion under the water or on the water. It can also be used to trigger underwater security cameras in order to visualize and document what is occurring.

## Fire Detection Systems

Almost all protection systems will include intrusion detection and fire safety in one integrated system. The fire protection system can be activated manually by use of a pull station should one smell or see smoke and fire. The pull station will activate the audible and visual strobe, fire protection enunciators in the building, and notify the central station and/or emergency dispatch for the fire department. In addition

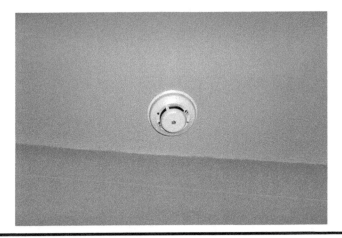

**Figure 6.4 Dual-chamber smoke detector. (Photograph by Daniel J. Benny.)**

to the manual pull station, there is a fire protection sensor that can be placed in the protected facility that will send an automatic signal to the central station or emergency dispatch for the fire department, and activate a set of audible and visual strobe fire protection enunciators.

The following fire protection sensors can be utilized:

*Dual-chamber smoke detector*—This sensor will provide early detection of smoke. It is used primarily for the protection of life, but early detection of a fire can also save property by providing early detection of a fire situation (Figure 6.4).

*Rate-of-rise heat detector*—This sensor is used in an area where a smoke detector cannot be used. This includes bathrooms and cooking areas where the normal activity in those areas would set off a smoke detector. The rate-of-rise heat detector will sense a rapid increase in the heat of an area due to a fire and will then activate the alarm system.

*Natural gas or carbon monoxide detector*—These two types of sensors are used to detect deadly gases that may build up in a facility. These sensors will provide early warning for evacuation.

*Water flow sensor*—For facilities that have a fire protection sprinkler system, this sensor will detect the drop in water pressure when the sprinkler is activated during a fire. This will result in an alarm being activated.

## Security Cameras

The use of security camera surveillance is very effective in the prevention of crime. It also allows for the documentation of events and provides evidence for an investigation should a crime occur. Security cameras can be utilized to provide protection from both external and internal theft (Figures 6.5 and 6.6).

Organizations may install security cameras at any location on the exterior of their property and in most all interior areas. The areas a security camera may not be utilized are in restrooms and locker rooms. Other than those locations, there is no expectation of privacy in the workplace. Key areas for the placement of security cameras include entrances and exits to all property buildings, and coverage of areas where property, goods, and sensitive information is stored. There should be outdoor coverage of parking areas and the grounds of the facility by security cameras.

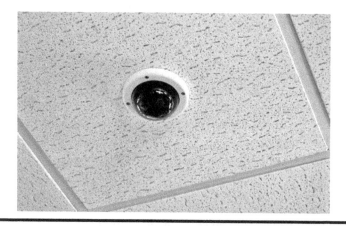

**Figure 6.5    Interior security camera. (Photograph by Daniel J. Benny.)**

**Figure 6.6    Exterior security camera. (Photograph by Daniel J. Benny.)**

The components of a security camera system include the lens/camera, transmission of the signal, monitoring, and recording.

## Lenses/Cameras

An effective security camera will require a low-light, variable lens so that it is adaptable to low-light situations. This is critical for security coverage inside facility structures and low-light areas. This will allow effective operations during both day and night hours. The camera should be color rather than black and white; color is critical in security applications. The camera should be housed in a protective cover and have the ability to be operated remotely to allow for zoom, pan, and tilt.

## Transmission of the Signal

Methods of transmitting the signal include the use of coaxial cable, fiber optics, the Ethernet, microwave, radio frequency radio, and laser. The best connection would be from coaxial cable, fiber optics, or the Ethernet. In situations where a direct line cannot be used due to distance and other factors, microwave, radio frequency radio, and laser can be used.

## Monitoring

Observation of the camera image can be viewed on a traditional television screen that should have a resolution of no less than 491 to 512 pixels with 580 lines. Images can also be viewed on desktop or laptop computers.

## Digital Recording and Monitoring

Digital recording and monitoring can be accomplished by the use of a digital recording system. Digital recording allows for the ability to store more information for a longer period of time depending on the server capacity. It also allows for obtaining stills from the video and the ability to enhance and enlarge them for identification and to share with law enforcement agencies. Another important feature of digital recording is that a time frame in the video can be searched by typing the date and time period. This makes retrieving and reviewing an important time event fast and easy. It can also be monitored remotely on a laptop computer (Figure 6.7).

## Motion Detection

Security cameras can be equipped to work in conjunction with motion detection sensors that activate the recording of the view of the camera only during the time of the activation by the motion sensor. The advantage of this is to save on the amount

**Figure 6.7** **A laptop computer being used remotely to monitor digital security cameras at Long Level Marina in Wrightsville, Pennsylvania. (Photograph by Daniel J. Benny.)**

of recorded time on a VHS tape when using the analog system or space on the server when using the digital system. It is most often used during the investigation of internal theft when the security department only needs to view an area when the sensor has been activated rather than going through hours of recording. For example, sonar placed underwater at ports can be used to activate an underwater security camera should they be approached.

## Determining Total System Costs

When determining the total security system cost there are several categories that must be explored. These include:

- System design costs
- System installation costs
- System operational costs
- Maintenance costs
- Information technology (IT) costs
- Replacement costs
- Return on the investment

It is important in the development of a security system that the total cost of the system be determined in order to develop a realistic budget that can be justified to top management and to ensure the system that is installed will meet the security requirements of the organization based on the threat.

## System Design Costs

Initially, there is the cost to develop the specifications for the project. This phase may require the assistance of a security consultant or engineer depending on the complexity and sophistication of the total security system. During this phase, an examination of the requirements includes the type of security system that would be the most effective based on the threat and location being protected, and the various components of the system. These system components can include an intrusion detection system central station server. It can also include the computer that will be utilized to operate the security system. The monitors that are required to work the system must also be included in the system design. Depending on the size and number of monitors, it may require the construction of a rack system to hold the monitors.

The various types, number, and placement of the security sensors will need to be determined and documented. As an example, this would include electronic door contacts or passive infrared sensors. The number and placement of fire sensors to include smoke detectors, heat detectors, and water flow sensors also need to be determined.

Access controls such as card readers, CyberLocks, traditional locks, and their placement in the facility must be identified. If electronic access control devices are utilized, conduit and wiring that is utilized to power the units will need to be calculated into the cost of the project.

The number and operating requirements of security cameras will need to be identified. This will include the lens, camera body, operating aspects such as zoom capabilities, and transmission method. Conduit and wiring that is utilized to power the units will need to be calculated into the cost of the project that will be integrated into the total security system that is being planned.

The design cost will also include development of the drawings and blueprints of the total system that is to be constructed and installed. There are, of course, the consultant fees for the individual or firm that is hired to design the security system. Cost for the engineer or engineering firm who will create the drawing and blueprints of the project must also be considered in the design process.

There are many aspects of the system design cost that must be taken into account. This will be important when submitting a budget for such a project. The life cycle of the security system should also be a consideration for long-term budget projection.

## System Installation Costs

One of the most expensive aspects of the entire security system project will be the system installation cost. This includes the cost of the products or components of the security system to include:

- Server
- Computer desk- or laptop

- Monitors
- Control panel
- Wiring
- Metal conduit
- Security cameras
- Camera brackets and housing

There is also the expense of the various sensors, such as door and window contacts, motion sensors, and fire protection sensors integrated into the system. If access control is part of the system, then there is the cost of the readers and cards to be used with the product.

Once the products have been identified and purchased, there will be the shipping cost to transport the system components to the installation site. This could include fees for rail and truck transport of large parts and the cost of local carriers for smaller products associated with the security system.

Labor costs for the individuals installing the system can be sizeable based on the local union or nonunion wages in the area. Laborers could include electricians, masons, carpenters, and painters.

Permits from the local government or municipality will be required in most cases for any new construction and electrical installations. The cost of the permits will vary based on the local governments and their specific requirements in which the facility and the security system project is located. Based on the nature of the product, there may also be state or Environmental Protection Agency permit fees to pay.

## System Operational Costs

Once the system is installed, there will be initial and ongoing system operation costs. In order to ensure the proper function of the system, current policies will need to be rewritten as well as the writing of new policies with regard to the operation of the security system. These operational changes may impact how other departments in the organizations operate, causing additional costs, to make such changes to the company operating policy and infrastructures.

Since all new security systems are computer based, there will be significant initial and ongoing support from the organization's IT department. This includes integrating the security system into the company IT system, the development of IT security procedures, and software to protect the system.

The increase in cost for electrical power is also part of the system operating cost. In the event of a power loss, the security system must function, so an emergency backup generator must be included in the ongoing cost.

The most expensive ongoing cost will include initial and continued training of the security staff and the wages for additional security staff to monitor the security system. In some cases, the addition of a comprehensive security system may free some security officers on patrol to monitor the system, but this is not the norm. In most all situations, additional security will need to be hired.

## Costs Related to Information Technology

When developing a new security system that is computer based, there will be IT-related costs. It is vital to know what IT systems are available on the corporate IP network. In the total cost of the security system, you will need to account for these cost factors associated with industry best practices for the management of IP-based technologies such as:

- Antivirus software
- Patch for the systems
- Management of the database
- Backup records
- Network bandwidth support

## Maintenance Costs

Keeping the system operating will require an investment in ongoing maintenance. This includes routine costs to keep the system hardware running and upgrades to the software. It will also require updates to the physical components of the system, such as wiring and mechanical functions.

If the system goes down in an emergency situation, there will be emergency repair and labor costs, especially if the breakdown occurs during the evening, weekend, or on a holiday when labor rates are higher. There will also be the labor costs for additional security and management staff to provide security coverage if the security system is not operating.

One method of reducing the cost of routine and emergency labor is to enter into an annual maintenance contract. It often will allow for a reduced rate for monthly or quarterly work on the security system, as well as emergency maintenance situations during the day, evenings, weekends, or holidays.

## Replacement Costs

All things will pass and that is true of security systems that become inoperable or antiquated. When designing and installing a new system, it is important to determine the life of the system. How long will it last before it needs to be replaced or becomes obsolete based on new hardware or software?

The manufacturer can most often advise on the life cycle of the system and potential future changes that may occur, along with a time frame for such changes. Based on the life expectancy projection, a long-term budget should be established so that there are funds for the replacement of the security system at the anticipated replacement time.

The life cycle of the security system should also be a consideration when a system is first selected.

## Cost–Benefit Analysis

When developing a security system, stakeholders must often prioritize requirements as part of the requirements engineering process. Not all aspects may be implemented due to lack of time, lack of resources, or changing or unclear project goals. It is important to define which requirements should be given priority over others.

## Cost of Loss

Computing cost of a security system can be very difficult. A simple cost calculation can take into account the cost of repairing or replacing the security system. Sophisticated cost calculations can factor in such variables as additional training required; the cost of having a system inoperable for a period of time; and any loss of customers, reputation, or clients as a result. Normally, assigning a cost range to each risk item is sufficient. One method to analyze the cost is to assign these costs based on a scale of loss as follows:

- Inoperable security systems over a short term (7–10 days)
- Inoperable security system over a medium term (1–2 weeks)
- Inoperable security system over a long term (more than 2 weeks)
- Permanent loss or destruction of the security system
- Accidental partial loss or damage of the security system
- Deliberate partial loss or damage of the security system
- Unauthorized disclosure within the organization

## Cost of Prevention

The cost of prevention includes calculating the cost of preventing each type of loss. This could include the cost to recover from

- Fire
- Power failure
- Terrorist incident

## Return on Investment

In all areas of management, to include the development of a total security system return on investment (ROI) is a critical step in selling the system to top management and obtaining funding for the project. A security investment such as a physical security system can enhance the security picture and an improved financial picture of the organization. Many security professionals have the technical security knowledge to sell a security system to top management but lack the ability to show how security improvements can contribute to a company's profitability.

Return on investment is a concept used to maximize profit to an organization for monies spent. It is used to determine the security system's financial worth. Return on investment is the annual rate of return on an investment.

Developing a security system can be complex. Return on investment can be measured using two basic criteria: costs and benefits. The object is to establish a credible return on investment and also to define a high-value security system project by the benefits that it provides.

## Cost Factors

There are common cost factors associated with the development of a security system. It is vital to estimate both the extent and timing of costs to be incurred during the security systems project. Typical cost factors for security systems may include the following:

- Security cameras/video
  - Cameras
  - Encoders
  - Fiber transceivers
  - Monitors
  - VCR/DVR/NVR and controls
  - Mass storage
- Access control
  - Counter panels
  - Doors and locks on panel
  - Card reader
  - Powered gates
  - Other security measures
- Communications
  - Leased line
- Cabling and power supplies
- Personnel associated with the security system
  - Receptionist
  - Credentialing
  - Contractor administration
  - Lock and key management
- Monitoring and control rooms
  - Alarm and video monitoring personnel
  - Operations support personnel
  - Physical security information management systems
  - Awareness and response of systems

- General system-related costs
  - Engineering and design of system
  - Infrastructure and maintenance
  - Software and licensing related to system
  - System deployment
  - Application integration
  - Administration and troubleshooting
  - User training

The return on investment can be justified based on the direct benefits attributable to the security system project. Direct benefits may include:

- Space improvements
- Wiring and communications infrastructure improvements
- Servers, applications, or systems improvements
- Storage increase
- Integration of systems such as security, fire protection, access control
- System maintenance and upgrades
- Training improvements

The following list is an example of indirect benefits/solutions:

- Visitor management administration and control
- Segregation of duties
- Parking permit administration
- Property pass administration
- Employee time keeping
- System troubleshooting and maintenance
- Alarm correlation and response
- Emergency communication and notification

Determining the total security systems cost is an important aspect in the development of the proposed security system. It aids in the approval of the security system and the funding for the security system project by top management.

## Locks, Key Control, and Access Control

The use of locks is one of the oldest forms of security. There are two general categories of locks: those that operate on mechanical concepts and those that use electricity to operate mechanical components of the locking system. Locks are used to secure personal doors, ships hatches, windows, utility ports, gates, file cabinets, and security containers in the protection of people, artifacts, books, and collections.

In addition to preventing access based on security concerns, locks can also prevent access to areas for safety-related issues. This might include securing hazardous materials storage areas, electrical rooms, engine rooms, and to lock out equipment on/off switches.

## Mechanical Locks

A mechanical lock utilizes physical moving parts and barriers to prevent the opening of the latch and includes the following parts: The latch or bolt that holds the door or window to the frame. The strike is the part into which the latch is inserted. The barrier is a tumbler array that must be passed by use of a key to operate the latch. The key is used to pass through the tumbler array and operate the latch or bolt.

## Wafer Tumbler Locks

The wafer tumbler lock utilizes flat metal tumblers that function inside the shell of the lock housing that creates a shear line. Spring tension keeps each wafer locked into the shell until lifted out by the key. The shell is matched by varying bit depths on the key (Figure 6.8).

## Dial Combination Locks

The dial combination lock is used on security containers, safes, and vaults, and is opened by dialing in a set combination. By eliminating a keyway, it provides a higher level of security. Although it does not utilize a key, the dial combination lock works on the same principle as the lever lock. By aligning gates on tumblers to allow insertion of the fence in the bolt, the lock can be opened by dialing in the assigned

**Figure 6.8    Low-security wafer tumbler padlock. (Photograph by Daniel J. Benny.)**

combination. The number of tumblers in the lock will determine the numbers to be used to open the combination lock.

## High-Security Dead Bolt Locks

The dead bolt lock is utilized for securing exterior and interior doors (Figures 6.9 through 6.12). The elements of the high-security dead bolt lock are the use of a restricted keyway so the key cannot be easily duplicated, a one-inch latch with

**Figure 6.9   Electronic keypad lock. (Photograph by Daniel J. Benny.)**

**Figure 6.10   Dead bolt lock. (Photograph by Daniel J. Benny.)**

**Figure 6.11   Dead bolt lock. (Photograph by Daniel J. Benny.)**

**Figure 6.12   Dead bolt lock with safety chain. (Photograph by Daniel J. Benny.)**

ceramic inserts so the latch cannot be forced open or cut, and tapered and rotating cylinder guards should be used so that a wrench cannot be used to remove the lock.

## Card Access Electrified Locks

An electrified lock permits doors to be locked and unlocked in a remote manner (Figures 6.13 and 6.14). It can be a simple push button near the lock or at a security central station, or work as part of a card proximity reader system or digital keypad. This system allows for the use of traditional electric latches or can be used with an electric high-security dead bolt system.

**Figure 6.13 Proximity card reader. (Photograph by Daniel J. Benny.)**

**Figure 6.14 Proximity card reader on a turnstile to control personnel access to a facility. (Photograph by Daniel J. Benny.)**

## Exit Locks

An exit lock or panic bars are used on doors designed as emergency exits from a building (Figure 6.15). They are locked from the outside but can be opened to exit the building by pushing on a bar that disengages the lock. Emergency doors should never be locked from the inside in any manner that would prevent immediate exit from the building.

## Master Locking Systems

When establishing a master locking system, it must be designed to meet the security needs of the owner or business. Without planning, the locking system will usually degrade to a system that is only providing privacy but not effective security. The goal is to make the locking system effective and user friendly so that the functions of the organization can continue unimpeded.

The following design criteria need to be considered in the development of a master locking system:

- *Number of locks*—This includes the total number of locks that will be installed on exterior and interior doors.
- *Categories of the locking system*—The categories of a locking system include exterior doors entering the building on the property; interior doors; high-security areas; combination locks for security containers and safes; and desk, computer, and file cabinet locks.

**Figure 6.15 Emergency door locking system. (Photograph by Daniel J. Benny.)**

## Control of Keys and Locking Devices

The security department, if there is one, or the business manager should control all keys and locking devices. This would include responsibility for the installation and repair of all locks, as well as maintaining the records of all keys made, issued, and collected.

## Master Keys

The master key, is a single key that fits all locks, must be controlled and secured by the security department or manager, and should not be removed from the property. This key may be signed out to members of the staff. It should only be issued once a day, and needs to be signed for and returned at the end of the shift when the security staff or top management leaves for the day. Submaster keys that allow access to specific areas may be issued for the term of employment to top management or security staff. The security department should keep a duplicate of all keys to the facility, desks, file cabinets, and access numbers to combination locks on security containers.

## Duplication of Keys

The duplication of company keys must be controlled. No key should be duplicated by the authorized locksmith without the authorization of the management or the security department.

## Lost Keys

Lost or misplaced keys are to be reported at once. An investigation into the circumstances related to the loss or misplacement of keys must be conducted.

## Disposition of Employee Keys upon Transfer or Termination

Upon the transfer of an employee or the termination of an employee, all keys that were issued must be returned and accounted for. This would include door, desk, and file cabinet keys issued to the employee.

# Security Containers

When protecting sensitive information, it is vital to have the documents or media stored in security containers or safes. These security containers should be high-quality commercial products (see Figure 6.16).

**Figure 6.16  Commercial Liberty safe. (Photograph by Daniel J. Benny.)**

When protecting U.S. government classified information, the security containers and safes must be security containers approved by the General Services Administration (GSA). All security containers that are approved by the GSA bear a "General Services Administration Approved Security Container" label affixed to the front of the security container and are classified as follows:

Class 1—The security container is insulated for fire protection. And the protection provided is
30 man-minutes against surreptitious entry
10 man-minutes against forced entry
1 hour protection against fire damage to content
20 man-hours against manipulation of the lock
20 man-hours against radiological attack

Class 2—The security container is insulated for fire protection and the protection provided is
20 man-minutes against surreptitious entry
1 hour protection against fire damage to contents
5 man-minutes against forced entry
20 man-hours against manipulation of the lock
20 man-hours against radiological attack
Class 3—The security container is uninsulated and the protection provided is
20 man-minutes against surreptitious entry
20 man-hours against manipulation of the lock
20 man-hours against radiological attack
No forced entry requirement
Class 4—The security container is uninsulated and the protection provided is
20 man-minutes against surreptitious entry
5 man-minutes against forced entry
20 man-hours against manipulation of the lock
20 man-hours against radiological attack
Class 5—The security container is uninsulated and the protection provided is
20 man-hours against surreptitious entry (increased from 30 man-minutes on containers produced after March 1991)
10 man-minutes against forced entry
20 man-hours against manipulation of the lock
20 man-hours against radiological attack
30 man-minutes against covert entry
Class 6—The security container is uninsulated and the protection provided is
20 man-hours against surreptitious entry
No forced entry test requirement
20 man-hours against manipulation of the lock
20 man-hours against radiological attack
30 man-minutes against covert entry

## Security Filing Cabinets

There are a variety of security filing cabinets manufactured to meet the standards of class 5 and class 6 security containers. Security filing cabinets are available in a variety of styles to include single, two, four, and five drawers, and in both letter-size and legal-size models.

# Security Barriers and Fencing

A security barrier can be anything that prevents vehicle or pedestrian access to the property or the facility and protected information. It may be natural barriers such as water, trees, or rock formations. These natural barriers may already be in place or can be placed on the property to provide a natural barrier (Figures 6.17 and 6.18). This is one of the aspects of what is known as crime prevention through environmental design (CPTED).

One of the most cost-effective barriers to secure the perimeter of a property or high-risk area such as fueling tanks is a chain-link fence (Figure 6.19). A chain-link fence is relatively low in cost and provides the flexibility to move it as needed. It also allows visibility beyond the property line by security, staff, and security cameras.

Chain-link fencing may not be used at some facilities because it is not aesthetically pleasing to look at. It may be used for some outdoor storage areas. Decorative fencing is often more aesthetically appealing and can provide adequate perimeter security (Figure 6.20).

If utilized, the security industry height for a fence is 6 feet with a 1 foot top guard mounted on a 45 degree angle facing away from the property constructed of barbed wire and/or razor ribbon. The fence must be secured in the ground by metal posts with bracing across the top and bottom of the fence. The opening in the fence should be no more than 2 inches.

With any fencing that is utilized for areas with vehicle access there should be at least two points of access in the event that one access is closed due to an emergency. All gates that are not used on a regular basis need to be secured with a high security padlock. The locked gate should also be equipped with a numbered security seal.

**Figure 6.17 Alcatraz Island, San Francisco, California, has water as a natural barrier. (Photograph by Daniel J. Benny.)**

Figure 6.18  Three Mile Island Nuclear Power Station, Middletown, Pennsylvania, has water as a natural barrier. (Photograph by Daniel J. Benny.)

Figure 6.19  Chain-link fence at Lakeside Marine, Harrisburg, Pennsylvania. (Photograph by Daniel J. Benny.)

**Figure 6.20  Decorative fencing at a White House gate. (Photograph by Daniel J. Benny.)**

This seal needs to be checked each day by security staff to ensure that the numbered seal is intact and matches the numbered seal placed on the gate. This will ensure that an unauthorized key is not being used so that a person can enter and exit the gate. It is also used to ensure that the original padlock on the gate was not cut off and replaced with a different lock, and then used by a perpetrator for continued unauthorized access into the secure area.

Access onto the property through the gate can be controlled by the use of a proximity access card and electric locking system on the gate. This can be used for vehicles or individuals.

Security fencing or netting can also be utilized underwater near docks and ships to prevent underwater access to facilities and watercraft. The underwater netting may be used long term or only during short-term high risk situations or threat levels.

Vehicle barriers can be used in conjunction with fencing and access control to prevent vehicles ramming through the access point (see Figure 6.21).

## Security Lighting

Security lighting is used to illuminate the perimeter of the property, gate access areas, walkways, and the vehicle parking area of the facility. The most effective security lighting is the sodium vapor (Figure 6.22).

**Figure 6.21** Hydraulic vehicle barrier used at 10 Downing Street, London, England, to prevent unauthorized vehicle access to the residence of the British prime minister. (Photograph by Daniel J. Benny.)

**Figure 6.22** Exterior security and emergency lighting. (Photograph by Daniel J. Benny.)

Lighting fixtures need to be placed in a security housing to prevent damage. The light can be mounted on posts and buildings. Lights can be activated by the use of a photoelectric cell that will automatically turn the light on at dusk and turn it off at dawn. This is more efficient than manually turning lights on and off each day. All light fixtures should be numbered for easy identification. This will be of value when reporting lights that are not working to ensure that they are repaired as quickly as possible.

These types of lighting devices include the following:

- Incandescent
- New fluorescent (to replace the incandescent)
- Quartz
- Mercury vapor
- Sodium vapor

## Incandescent

Incandescent is what is known as the common light bulb or flood light that is being phased out. It has been used to provide illumination at doorways and to direct light to a building at night. It is suitable for security for a single building but is not considered for security lighting of large facilities. This is due to the high energy cost and low illumination that it provides.

## New Fluorescent (to Replace the Incandescent)

The new fluorescent lights are used to provide illumination at doorways and to direct light to a building at night and are replacing the incandescent bulb. As with all florescent lighting it is not suitable for industrial use. This is due to the low illumination that it provides.

## Quartz

The quartz light provides better illumination and emits a white light. It is instantaneously activated when turned on and has been used to light parking areas. It does have a high energy cost.

## Mercury Vapor

The mercury vapor light provides good illumination and emits a white light. It does require a warm-up time and cannot be instantaneously activated when turned on. It is used to light parking areas and roadways. It has a lower energy cost than the previously mentioned lights.

## Sodium Vapor

The sodium vapor light is considered the best for security. It will light instantaneously and has a lower energy cost than all other security lighting. It has excellent penetration at night and in fog due to the amber light. The amber light can distort color on security cameras and upon viewing objects by the security officer.

# Protection of Windows and Utility Ports

All facilities will have windows that will require protection. The first security consideration for window protection is the window itself or what is called glazing. That is, the type of glass or plastic that is used as a window. The more security that is required, the stronger the glazing should be. The stronger the glazing, the more expensive it will be. What is used will be based on the threat assessment and if there are any interior intrusion detection systems being used in the structure.

Window areas can be made of glass, acrylic, or what is known as Lexan. The following is a list of the glass, acrylic, and Lexan products that can be used for non-bullet resistance protection:

- Annealed glass
- Wire-reinforced glass
- Tempered glass
- Laminated glass
- Annealed glass (with security film)
- Acrylic
- Lexan

## Annealed Glass

Annealed glass, also known as windowpane glass, breaks very easily and provides the least amount of protection of all of the glazing materials. It breaks into shards of glass that are very sharp and can be used as weapons. These shards can cause injury to individuals in the area if the glazing material is broken by a perpetrator or explosive blast.

## Wire-Reinforced Glass

Wire-reinforced glass is annealed glass with wire imbedded into the glazing. While it looks as if it adds security, it does not and is easily broken. The one advantage is that the glass will not break in large shards, as the wire will hold the broken glass together.

## Tempered Glass

Tempered glass is a stronger material but can be defeated easily. When broken, it breaks into small pieces of glass that are relatively harmless. This glass was used in older vehicle windshields.

## Laminated Glass

Laminated glass is coated with plastic. It also can be easily defeated. When broken, it holds the glass together in large harmless sheets. This is what is used in vehicle windshields.

## Annealed Glass (with Security Film)

Annealed glass with a security film has a layer of acrylic between two layers of glass. It is difficult to break through this glazing and is the best of the glass products for security protection when bullet resistance is not a requirement.

## Acrylic

Acrylic is a plastic and offers little protection. It also breaks into large shards if broken. It scratches easily and will discolor over time due to sunlight.

## Lexan

Lexan is the trademark name of a glazing that is impregnable to breakage and is the best of all the security glazing when bullet resistance is not a requirement. Where bullet resistance is required due to a high threat of robbery or terrorist attack by firearm or explosive devices, the following bullet-resistant material can be utilized:

- Bullet-resistant glass
- Bullet-resistant acrylic
- Lexgard

Bullet-resistant glass is a glass glazing that can be from 1/4 inch to 1 inch in thickness. The thicker the glass, the more protection it provides from small arms weapons. It will stop most bullets, but it does cause spalling. Spalling is when the bullet is trapped in the glass and a small particle of glass breaks off and flies in the direction away from where the bullet was fired. This can cause injury to anyone near the bullet resistant glass.

Bullet-resistant acrylic is an acrylic glazing that can be from 1/4 inch to 1 inch in thickness. The thicker the glazing, the more protection it provides from small arms weapons. It will stop most bullets, but it does cause spalling.

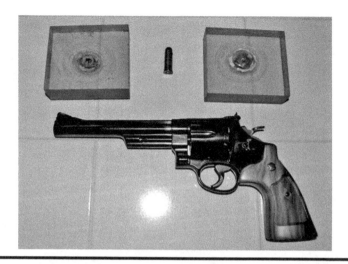

**Figure 6.23 Lexgard bullet-resistant glazing shot with a Smith & Wesson .44 Magnum. (Photograph by Daniel J. Benny.)**

Lexgard is the trademark name of an acrylic glazing (Figure 6.23). The glazing at 1 inch thickness is the best protection from firearms and explosive devices, and will stop all small arms weapons and most rifles. With Lexgard, there will be no spalling. This is a product that one would find on the presidential limousines used by the Secret Service.

Window protection can also be provided with the use of security bars or steel screening placed over the windows. The bars and screens should be securely mounted into the window frame. It is important to make sure that the use of bars and steel screens on the windows do not impede access out of the structure in the event of an emergency evacuation.

Utility ports are areas of access into the port facilities such as water, air vents, and trash. These areas can be protected with bars, locks, and intrusion detection systems. Use of security cameras are recommended for trash compactor areas.

# Radio-Frequency Identification, Magnetometers, and X-Rays

Physical security measures can be of value in the protection of property when used at the entrance and exit of a property. The concept is to use a security device that is placed on the materials to be protected and to have security detection as well as a detection device that is typically located at all exits. Magnetic media should be able to safely pass by or through any detection device and such devices should be equipped with audible or visible alarms, or both.

**Figure 6.24  Electromagnetic detection system. (Photograph by Daniel J. Benny.)**

There are two primary methods currently used for detection: electromagnetic detection and radio frequency identification (Figure 6.24). These technological solutions can prevent, reduce, and detect theft of property. Of the two methods, the most effective is the radio frequency identification. The advantage of this system is that it does not require line of sight to be read. The tags can be placed on any type of property or media, including CDs and DVDs.

## Magnetometers

Used at the entrance and exit of the property, a magnetometer, also known as a metal detector, is a physical security device that responds to metal that may not be readily apparent by direct observation. In metal detectors, an oscillator produces an alternating current. This current passes through a coil, thus producing an alternating magnetic field, such that if some form of conductive metal is near the coil, "eddy" currents are produced. This produces another such alternating magnetic field that is subsequently detected, thus alerting any user to the presence of a metallic object. This can be used to detect the removal of metal objects from the property or from individuals bringing items inside facilities such as weapons or tools that could be used to defeat a physical security system once inside.

## X-Rays

The x-ray is used at the entrance and exit of a property to inspect cases, handbags, or packages entering or leaving the property. It is used to detect contraband, weapons, and explosives entering the facility or items being removed. The use of an x-ray in most cases will deter such activity and can of course detect such attempts.

## *Expert Witnesses*

Private investigators with security expertise may be court-qualified to provide expert testimony on security matters, such as security administration, security force management, physical security maritime security, aviation security use of force, and firearms. Both plaintiffs and defendants in civil cases relating to the inadequacy of security utilize expert witnesses in the security profession. An individual may be the victim of a crime on private property and then sue the owner of that property for failure to protect them by not providing adequate security in the form of security equipment or personnel in this civil matter.

## Technical Surveillance Countermeasures

Technical surveillance countermeasures refers to the profession of detecting, identifying, and removing eavesdropping devices that are recording or transmitting conversations or sending real-time video to unauthorized individuals for the purpose of industrial espionage. The private investigator can offer this service to clients in the protection of their privacy and information. This service is vital in a counterespionage investigation. The use of technical surveillance countermeasures needs to be considered as part of every counterespionage program.

The detection of eavesdropping devices is not as simple as it used to be. It is not a matter of just looking behind photos or under a lamp to locate a listening device. With new technology, such surveillance devices are miniature and easily concealed in everyday objects. Detecting such devices requires the use of complex technical surveillance countermeasures, technical services, and equipment. Many organizations will hire a private investigator to conduct technical surveillance countermeasures.

The private investigator can obtain technical surveillance countermeasures equipment and the cost will vary. Research Electronics International is one of the most prestigious suppliers of this equipment. A countermeasures package, for about $4000, can detect and locate sophisticated eavesdropping transmitters, both digital and analog to include radio frequency audio, video, and data units (Figure 6.25). It will also detect infrared and carrier current transmitters. The package allows for the testing of telephone and miscellaneous wiring for monitoring devices. Research Electronics International also provides classroom and practical exercise training on all of the technical surveillance countermeasures it sells.

A private investigator trained in the use of technical surveillance countermeasures equipment can charge between $2000 and $5000, depending on the perceived or known threat and area to be swept for monitoring devices. An electronic

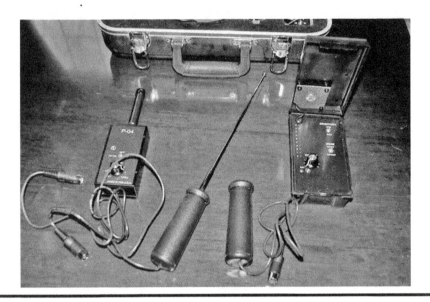

**Figure 6.25  Technical surveillance countermeasures kit. (Photograph by Daniel J. Benny.)**

sweep can be conducted in a time frame of a few hours to several days, depending on the number of rooms and areas that need to be swept and protected. The more areas to sweep, the higher the fee to the client.

By utilizing technical surveillance countermeasures as part of their services, the private investigator can increase their workload and profit. More important, it will allow the private investigator to be of more value to their existing and future clients.

Technical surveillance countermeasures sweeps should be done on a regular basis, but based on a random schedule. Surprise sweeps should also be conducted. These surprise sweeps are very effective in the detection and prevention of eavesdroppers. Locations in the organization that are recommended for technical surveillance countermeasures sweeps include the following:

- Executive offices of the president/CEO
- Executive residences
- Transportation modalities (corporate cars, aircraft, boats)
- Executive mobile phones
- Executive home phones (landlines)
- Corporate board rooms
- Off-site corporate business meeting rooms
- Corporate security office

Depending on the size of the facility, other areas may also be included in a scheduled sweep. If there is an indication of a threat from unauthorized monitoring, then a technical surveillance countermeasures sweep should be done at once. Some of the indicators that information is being compromised through such monitoring may be any of the following:

- Loss of a bid that should have been won
- Unexplained reduction in company sales
- Corporate strategies made public
- Competitor's knowledge of company pricing and sales strategy
- Issues with labor contract negotiations
- Theft of protected information and trade secrets
- Confidential employee records released
- Release of financial information about the company

Offering technical surveillance countermeasure services to clients will make the private investigator more versatile and increase the private investigator's professional presence and increase business profits.

## Polygraphs

The polygraph is an excellent tool that can be used by the private investigator for specific types of investigations. It is a violation of federal law to use the polygraph for preemployment background investigations in the private sector, with the exception of the private drug industry. Public law enforcement and the federal government can use the polygraph during the job application process. The investigator could use the polygraph in the investigation of internal theft or espionage, domestic situations, or to even verify a client's or witness's claim of innocence.

The polygraph measures several physical areas of the body that are associated with and respond to the activity of the mind. These include perspiration, heart rate, and breathing. A sensor is placed on the fingertip to measure perspiration. A cuff is placed on the arm to measure blood pressure. An expandable tube is placed around the chest to measure breathing.

As questions are asked and responded to, what the test subject is thinking about the question and how they respond to the question will be recorded based on the body's physical reaction to the question. When one is being deceptive, sweating and the heart rate increase, and breathing becomes heavier. This is what is measured by the polygraph. The results must then be read and interpreted by the polygraph examiner.

The polygraph is not an exact science and it is not admissible in a court of law. It is, however, an effective tool in some investigations that can guide the private investigator in the right direction or confirm what the private investigator may already know. If the private investigator becomes certified and purchases a polygraph, it is a service that can be offered to clients.

## Protective Service

Protective service involves providing protection or bodyguard service to a client. Depending on the ability and scope of the investigator and the organization, the protective service may range from a protective escort involving the investigator and the client to a comprehensive protective service detail providing protection for numerous individuals at various locations. This is a vital service that a private investigator can provide as it relates to homeland security.

The role of a private investigator in conducting protective service will depend on the requirements of the client and the threat level against the client. The protective service most often will include what is called close protection. This is when the protective agent provides continuous security escort for the client. The goal of a protective service assignment is to protect the client, also known as the "principle" in the protective service profession, from all threats. This includes threats caused by personal design, accident, or negligence. Absolute protection is never possible so the objective of a protective service assignment is to operate in a manner that minimizes the risk of an attack on the principle and its chances of success.

Protective service is a critical element of homeland security and is one area that the trained private investigator can contribute to in this effort. The goal of the protective service operation is to

- Prevent any injury or death to the principle, be it accidental or intentional
- Prevent kidnapping
- Prevent any possible embarrassment to the principle when in public
- Ensure that the protective service does not hinder the principle's schedule

### Appearance

When the private investigator is working a protective service operation, the investigator must always look professional and fit into the environment of the principle. If the principle is dressed in formal attire, the private investigator must also dress formal; if the principle is dressed casual, then the private investigator must be dressed casual. The private investigator should always be well groomed and needs to adapt to the style and setting of the principle.

### Media

When dealing with the media on a protective service detail, it is essential not to permit the press to interfere with the safety and security of the principle. Direct all media inquiries with regard to the principle to the public relations staff member of the principle. Always be tactful and professional but firm when dealing with the media. If the media is to enter a secure area, all press credentials must be checked, as well as baggage and equipment.

## Threat Assessments

Based on the situation, threats to the principle can be critical. All threats need to be taken seriously and must continue to be assessed. The threat may be specific against the principle, or it could be more general because of the proximity of the principle to a potential threat. There will be concerns based on locations that are known to be high-crime or a hostile environment.

To counter any threat, a threat assessment must be conducted. The goal of the assessment is to determine if there is a potential threat to the principle based on the locations they will travel and visit. How much protection that is provided will be determined on the threat assessment.

# Investigative Photography

The private investigator does not provide crime scene photography, as this is the role of public law enforcement. A private investigator may be asked to photograph a nonactive scene of a crime or accident well after the event has occurred to support a criminal defense or civil litigation trial. The private investigator will most often use investigative photography to document the activity of an individual or activity around a location by means of surveillance.

Investigative photography during a surveillance job may be to document criminal activity at a location. The photographs may be used to gather evidence with regard to criminals and terrorists. Photographs can be used to document fraud activity of individuals, such as workers' compensation for the insurance industry. Investigative photographs may also be used to document infidelity in civil cases as well as violations of child custody orders and issues related to cohabitation.

The private investigator needs to have proficiency in the use of photographic equipment to ensure that usable photographs will be taken. The private investigator also needs the tactical skill to be able to take clandestine photographs during surveillance activity, so that the private investigator is not recognized. The conditions in the field will be diverse including low-light, darkness, or inclement darkness situations.

Clandestine surveillance photography is incredibly challenging. The private investigator often works under field conditions that can be so disparaging that others may not even attempt it. Photographs must be taken at times from long distances under adverse lighting and weather conditions, traversing and occupying inhospitable terrain. Based on the case, the private investigator may be attempting to obtain photography evidence in an active countersurveillance environment.

Unlike other types of photography, such as commercial or even family photography, the private investigator will not have the cooperation of the subject of the photography or the location where the photography will occur. The location can be difficult and range from a crowded urban area to a desolate country setting. The subject may also be moving fast on foot or traveling in a motor vehicle. The subject must be unaware that the pictures are being taken.

There are situations where the private investigator may not be able to conceal themselves in order to take the photograph. In such situations, the private investigator must resort to using a pretext to take the photograph out in the open so the subject does not suspect that they are the target of the photograph. The subject will see the private investigator taking photographs in the area but must believe they are for an unrelated reason. For example, I once had to photograph a man and a woman meeting in a public park. Due to the location it was not possible to be concealed to take the photograph. While the two subjects were together on a blanket in the park, I walked to a park pavilion next to the subjects with a camera and a clipboard. I acted as if I were inspecting the pavilion and made notes on the clipboard. I then began to take photographs of the pavilion from all angles that in the end included the two individuals together in the park. They had no clue that they were the subject of the photography until I testified in court on the matter.

The equipment used by the private investigator is of singular importance. While a camera on a mobile phone may work in some close situations, it is not acceptable investigative photography equipment. A digital single-lens camera that can be used in automatic or manual mode should be used. The private investigator should also have various lenses to use for wide-angle or long-distance photography, such as a 400 mm to 500 mm lens. Night vision lenses will be required for investigative photography in low-light and night conditions. For taking a photograph at a long distance and at night, a tripod should be considered. A tripod with expandable legs needs to be acquired so that it can sit on a tabletop or on the ground for proper use.

Aerial investigative photography is often used to document large areas on the ground related to an investigation, such as a road intersection for an accident investigation. For aerial photography, the private investigator would need access to an aircraft either by holding a Federal Aviation Administration private pilot certificate or hiring a pilot to fly the private investigator to the area to be photographed. As a pilot and aircraft owner, the author has used his aircraft numerous times for such photography related to investigations, expert witness work, and security consulting.

## Process Services

In those states that authorize private investigators to serve legal processes, this is an additional service that can be offered, especially to clientele in the legal profession. The private investigator will or attempt to serve the assigned legal documents. The private investigator making the service will then report back the results, that is, if the service was or was not made in the form of a signed affidavit.

# Shopping Services

Shopping services are similar to undercover investigations but are greatly limited in scope. The private investigator is retained by a retail or service business, such as a store, movie theater, or restaurant, to shop at the business or utilize its services under the pretense of being a customer. The private investigator will be alert to activity on the part of the employees with regard to theft of company property or funds, effective service to customers, and adherence to company policies. The maintenance of the worksite, including its general appearance and safety considerations, will also be noted during the investigation. The private investigator then reports back to the client on the findings of the shopping service. Conducting such a covert investigation may identify activity other than theft or failure to perform required duties, such as activity related to homeland security threats. Employees may be using the business to further contacts and other activity related to terrorism.

# Penetration Checks

Penetration checks involve the utilization of a private investigator by a business to determine if the company's security defenses or procedures can be breached. This is to test the security of the facility to determine if the system and procedures in place will prevent or detect crime and terrorism. This does not mean that the investigator attempts to break into a business circumventing physical security devices. It does involve the investigator trying to gain access to the business to include access to sensitive areas by talking or intimidating his or her way past employees. It is merely a test to see if employees, whether they are security personnel or regular staff, are alert and performing their duties in an efficient manner.

With regard to homeland security, the investigator might not attempt to enter the facility, but instead act in the manner a terrorist would if gathering intelligence on the facility as a possible target. This tests if the security or other company staff notice the possible signs of terrorism and report or investigate it.

# Bibliography

Baker, P. and D. J. Benny. *Complete Guide to Physical Security*. Boca Raton, FL: CRC Press, 2012.

Fischer, R. J. and G. Green. *Introduction to Security*. Burlington, MA: Elsevier, 2012.

U.S. Coast Guard. *USCG Protective Service Manual*. Washington, DC: U.S. Government Printing Office, 1999.

# Chapter 7

# Private Investigative Agencies and Security Services

Many private investigative agencies provide uniformed security services to clients based on state licensing requirements. In some states it is a combined license, and in others one must have a private investigator license and a security officer license to conduct both types of services. When establishing a security service, the hiring of a security professional as the chief security officer (CSO) is the first priority. The selection of this individual is critical to the success of the operation of the security department. The chief security officer should report to the principle owner of the investigative agency. The individual selected should have at minimum a bachelor's degree in security administration or criminal justice from an accredited university or college, with a master's or doctorate preferred.

A security professional with professional security certification should also be considered. There are several security-related certifications that are of value to the chief security office. One professional security certification, Certified Protection Professional (CPP), is offered by ASIS International. This designation is accepted nationally and internationally by the security profession. CPP has been established for individuals working in security supervision and management. Upon successful completion of the comprehensive exam, one must have years of security work experience and/or a college degree.

## Determining the Size of the Security Department

Once the chief security officer is hired, that individual must work with the owner of the investigative agency to make a determination with regard to the size of the security force that will be required. The need for a security department must be established and will be based on the number of clients the agency has, the type of contracts, and locations of the contracts. In the end it will be based on the needs of the clients.

Additional needs will be based on a physical security survey of the client's property to be protected by the security force. The duties and functions of the security force at the client property must be considered based on the security threat. The physical security survey and the physical security measures to be utilized at the property will have an impact on the number of security officers that will be required to provide adequate protection.

The use of intrusion detection systems, security cameras, security lights, fire protections systems, and access controls such as proximity card readers may reduce the number of security officers required to patrol the property. If there are no or limited physical security measures, there will be a requirement to establish a larger security force in order to effectively secure the location to be protected. The use of more physical security measures may allow for the reduction of the size of the force. Regardless of the level of physical security protection, there will in most all cases be a need for security officers to monitor the intrusion, fire, access control, and camera systems. There is also the requirement for security officers to be able to respond to the various alarms or activity observed on security cameras.

For each security post to be covered 24 hours a day, the maritime organization will need to hire four security officers to account for days off, holidays, and vacation. So, if two security officers are required to be on duty 24 hours a day, there would be a requirement to hire eight security officers.

## Mission of the Security Force

In determining the size of the security force, the mission and duties of the security department must be determined. The primary duty of a security force is to provide proactive patrols of the property in order to protect life and prevent losses, respond to emergencies, and provide assistance to staff and visitors.

The security patrols may be conducted by foot patrol within the buildings and on the property. Outdoors in parking areas the use of vehicles such as automobiles with all-wheel drive capabilities, bicycles, or Segways, may be used. If the client is a port facility, then small watercraft may be utilized to patrol waterways near the port facility and docks. Small watercraft may also be deployed to provide security around ships at port.

The security force should be utilized to control access to the property. The access control may begin at the perimeter of the property and at vehicle entrances. This would include checking the identification cards issued by the client. The security force would also be responsible for inspecting vehicles entering the facility, if necessary. Access control points required to be covered by security officers may also include pedestrian entrances. Escorts are often provided by the security force for visitors into restricted areas. These escorts could also be for the transportation of money, high-value property, or confidential company information. The escorts may take place on the property and off, such as the case of a money escort to a banking facility. Providing security escorts to employee parking areas for employees leaving work during hours of darkness may also be a service that is provided by the security force.

Inspections of the facility for security threats, safety, and loss hazards are a function that should be performed by security officers while on patrol. Depending on the size of the property and the number of buildings to be patrolled, this may be a duty that would be performed by security officers on patrol.

Investigations of losses, safety issues, accidents, violations of regulations, and employee misconduct and criminal activity, and possible terrorism will require the attention of investigators if there is a significant caseload based on the size and population of the facility. In most cases, this function would be conducted by the chief security officer.

Monitoring of intrusion detection and fire safety systems, security cameras, and access control points is an important function of security. The establishment of a proprietary security communications and monitoring center to dispatch security staff; answer security-related calls; and monitor the security, fire safety, cameras, and access control points will require the hiring of additional security officers. These positions should be staffed by trained security officers who can be rotated between patrol functions and monitoring duties. This is critical since a trained security officer will be more effective at responding to security calls and situations arising while monitoring the security and safety systems than a person hired to only work in the communications center. It is also important to not have an individual monitor such systems for more than 2 hours. A security officer will become less effective at monitoring a security camera if the assignment lasts more than 2 hours. For example, by having security officers working in the maritime land-based communications center, they can be rotated to the patrol function after 2 hours in the communications center.

The final function to consider is the administrative duties associated with a security force. These duties will include securing security staff records, reports, and payroll, and other administrative duties that may be required.

Based on a review of all the possible duties and functions of a security force that have been described, a final determination can be made of what services and duties the security force will perform.

## Legal Authorization

The private investigative agency owner and the chief security officer must know the state laws relating to policies on apprehension of suspects. Review all state laws before making any citizen's arrest for any criminal offense. This enforcement is accomplished through the writing of reports and verbal directions or commands as the situation warrants.

Security officers have the authority to stop anyone on the property where they are assigned for the purpose of identifying such persons or determining if he or she is authorized to be in a specific area. The officers may also stop anyone to investigate a suspicious activity or to obtain information regarding an individual whom they believe has committed a criminal offense.

An arrest is the taking of a person into custody in order that he or she may be held to answer for or be prevented from committing a criminal offense. A citizen's arrests in most states can only be made for felonies committed in the presence of the security officer and for the safety and protection of life.

The crime codes and other laws relating to the authority of security officers of each state in which a facility is located must be consulted. Each security officer should be responsible for knowing and understanding the state laws and must be trained in this area.

## Pedestrian Stops

Security officers should be authorized to stop anyone on the client's property with probable cause to ascertain their identity and purpose for being at the facility. Probable cause includes individuals acting in a suspicious manner, loitering around for periods of time, and individuals seen in unauthorized areas or during periods the facility is closed to the public.

All staff at facilities should be required to have a photo identification card in their possession while on duty and should be required to wear it in appropriate areas or show it upon request. Should an unidentifiable person be stopped and refuse to show identification, they should be escorted off the property. Any pedestrian stop should be documented in the security officer's daily activity report. Should the stop be the result of a significant incident, an incident report should be completed.

## Profile and Security Threats

A review of the profile of the facility to be protected is necessary when determining the size of the security force. The type of operation of the facility with regard to its size, hours of operation, number of employees, visitors, as well as security threats are key elements that must be considered to make a determination as to the size of the security force.

The security threat will be based on numerous factors to include the type of property and location. The local crime rate and previous crime and losses against the facility must also be evaluated to determine the current risk.

## Size of the Facility

The size of the facility including the square footage of buildings and the number of floors in the buildings must be calculated in determining the number of security officers required to provide adequate protection.

## Hours of Operation

Hours of operations of the facility will impact the security force size to provide adequate security coverage. If open 8 to 5 each day, a detection system can be used at night, and it obviously will require less security force coverage than a period of longer operations. As hours of operation lessen or expand based on the specific situation, the level of security coverage will also need to be adjusted.

## Number of Employees and Visitors

The number of employees will have an impact on the size of the security force. The number may change by day of the week and hours of the day, and need to be calculated into the security coverage for the facility.

# Contract Security Force

The advantage of the private investigative agency offering a contract security force service to clients is that there is the flexibility to hire full or part time or a combination of both for whatever length of time required. The client company utilizing the contract security officer does not need to place ads to recruit, interview, or hire the officers. It is less expensive because the licensed private investigator contractor firm pays for the benefits, training, equipment, and uniforms of the security officers. Another advantage is that contract security officers are easy to terminate. If an officer is not performing well, the security contractor can remove them from the property and replace them with another security officer.

## Security Force Uniforms and Identification

Traditionally, security officers wear a uniform. A uniform is a symbol of authority and allows the security officer to be easily identified during an emergency or when assistance is required by staff or visitors to an organization. The most common security uniform is slacks and a short or long sleeve police-/military-style shirt with a security patch, name tag, and a badge where authorized by state or local laws.

During colder weather, there are a variety of light- and heavy-weight water-resistant jackets and coats that can be utilized. Patches, name tags, and badges are also placed on the outer garment for ease of identification. Headwear is also part of the security uniform and can be a more formal eight-point cap, trooper hat, or ball cap style with badge or security insignia placed on the front of the headwear.

A softer uniform image may be selected rather than the traditional security uniform. It often consists of a jacket, tie, and slacks that may have a security patch attached with a name tag. Where permitted by law, a security badge may be displayed on the jacket using a pocket holder. In warmer seasons or climates, the softer uniform may be slacks with a shirt and tie or a polo-type shirt with security patches, name tag, and badge. The security attire may be business dress or business casual rather than a distinctive uniform. If this type of clothing is utilized, a name tag and security badge in a pocket holder should be utilized for easy identification as a security officer.

Just as the security uniform provides a symbol, so does security department identification. Badges, where authorized by state and local law, are a universally recognized symbol of authority. Shoulder patches also add to the authority of the security officer and identify the company or contract agency with whom they are employed. The most important aspect of security identification is a photo identification card to be worn on the uniform or carried in a case. This will provide for positive identification of the security officer where they work.

Security uniforms and identification allow the security officer to be identified as an authority figure, but uniforms and identification alone do not provide the security officer with such authority. The authority must come from legal codes that apply to the security officer depending on the state in which they operate. The authority also comes from the organization for which they are employed. This legitimacy must also be based on the proper use of such authority.

## Security Force Protective Equipment

Where authorized by state law, protective equipment may be considered for the security department. The type of protective equipment utilized will be based on the threat level, location, and mission of the security force, and may range from handcuffs to the carrying of firearms. Many states require specialized training before being authorized to carry various types of protective equipment. In Pennsylvania, for example, security officers who carry a baton or firearm must complete what is known as the Lethal Weapons Act 235 Course. To attend the 40-hour course, the student must submit to a criminal background check, and medical and psychological evaluations. The 40-hour course covers the legal aspects of carrying a weapon, the authority of a security officer, use-of-force considerations, and the Pennsylvania Crimes Code. Students must pass a written test and qualify on the firing range to become certified under the Lethal Weapons Act. It is important to know the requirements with regard to carrying a weapon in the state in which security officers are operating to ensure compliance with the laws of the state.

Handcuffs are important should the security officer be required to make a citizen's arrest in the performance of their duties. Handcuffs provide a means to secure an individual who becomes violent either before or after a citizen's arrest. The use of handcuffs in such situations provides for the safety of the security officer and the public. Handcuffs should be of good quality and have the capability of being double locked. The double locking mechanism prevents the handcuffs from being tightened on the suspect by accident or by the suspect to then claim an injury from their use.

Oleoresin capsicum (or OC spray or pepper spray) is a lachrymatory irritant agent that can be carried by security officers. It provides a nonlethal method of self-defense for the security officer and is very effective in most situations. Security officers should be certified by the manufacturer of the oleoresin capsicum product to ensure proper use and for liability purposes.

Batons have been carried by security for over a hundred years and they can be used as both a defensive and offensive protective tool. When used offensively, they are considered a deadly weapon. Batons come in various styles to include the traditional striate baton, the collapsible ASP baton, and the PR-24 full size or collapsible model (Figure 7.1). Certification should be obtained by the manufacturer of the particular baton that is carried for proper use and liability protection.

Firearms may be carried by the security department based on the legal requirements of the state. The threat and mission of the security department at a particular

**Figure 7.1   PR-24 baton and ASP baton. (Photograph by Daniel J. Benny.)**

site must also be considered. If a security officer carries a firearm, they must be equipped with alternate means of protective equipment such as a baton and oleoresin capsicum. This provides the security officer with a nonlethal response option if use of deadly force would not be authorized based on the situation.

A revolver or semiautomatic firearm may be carried (Figures 7.2 through 7.4). In some situations security officers may also carry a shotgun (Figure 7.5). In addition to state legal requirements for qualification and certification to carry a firearm, security officers should be trained and qualify with the weapons and ammunition they carry at least once a year. Many security departments require such training and qualification twice and up to four times a year.

**Figure 7.2    Sig Sauer 9 mm Model 228 and Glock 9 mm Model 19 Gen4 are examples of semiautomatic pistols used by security forces. (Photograph by Daniel J. Benny.)**

**Figure 7.3    Sig Sauer 9mm Model M11-A1 used by security forces. (Photograph by Daniel J. Benny.)**

**Figure 7.4** Smith & Wesson .44 Magnum and various Colt .38 and .32 Cal revolvers that have been used by private investigators in the performance of their duties. (Photograph by Daniel J. Benny.)

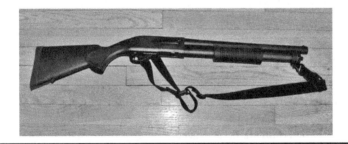

**Figure 7.5** Remington 870 12 gauge tactical shotgun. (Photograph by Daniel J. Benny.)

## Use of Force Options

■ Security officer presence—No force is used. Considered the best way to resolve a situation.
  – The mere presence of a security officer works to deter crime or diffuse a situation.
  – Security officers' attitudes are professional and nonthreatening.

■ Verbalization—Force is not physical.
  - Security officers issue calm, nonthreatening commands, such as "Let me see your identification."
  - Security officers may increase their volume and shorten commands in an attempt to gain compliance. Short commands might include stop or don't move.
■ Empty-hand control—Security officers use bodily force to gain control of a situation.
  - Soft technique—Security officers use grabs, holds, and joint locks to restrain an individual.
  - Hard technique—Security officers use punches and kicks to restrain an individual.
■ Less-lethal methods—Security officers use less-lethal technologies to gain control of a situation.
  - Blunt impact—Security officers may use a baton to immobilize a combative person.
  - Chemical—Security officers may use chemical sprays or projectiles embedded with chemicals to restrain an individual.
■ Lethal force—Security officers use lethal weapons to gain control of a situation. Should only be used if a suspect poses a serious threat to the security officer or another individual.
  - Security officers use deadly weapons such as firearms or baton striking of a vital area of the body (head, neck, kidney, or groin) to stop an individual's actions.

## Security Force Vehicles

The security force may maintain and operate patrol vehicles for use at client facilities and for other client needs. Based on the size of the property and climate conditions, an automobile may be used or a four-wheel drive vehicle may be selected. The vehicles should be visibly marked in accordance with state law.

## Security Force Communications

Several means of communication should be available to the security force to ensure immediate and effective communication during both routine and emergency situations. These should include portable two-way radios and mobile two-way radios if there are security vehicles on the property (see Figure 7.6). The use of mobile telephone by security officers is also recommended for emergency communications.

When using any form of communication, members of the security force are expected to communicate in a professional and service-oriented manner. When

**Figure 7.6 Security force communications: telephone, mobile phone, and security radio. (Photograph by Daniel J. Benny.)**

using two-way radios, Federal Communications Commission (FCC) guidelines must be adhered to. At no time while talking on any type of communications equipment should members of the security force utilize CB or other types of slang or jargon, nor should profanity be used on the security force communication system.

## Security Force Reports

In order to document incidents, complaints, and activities in which the security department becomes involved, various reports will be required. All reports should to be written on a computer if possible. The use of a typewriter or hand printed in ink using block letters is acceptable.

Completed security reports are to be considered legal documents, as they may be utilized in criminal, civil, governmental, or cultural property proceedings. Reports and the information contained in them must be protected.

### Incident/Complaint Report and Continuation Report

The incident/complaint report form should be utilized to document all important incidents that occur on the property and any complaints received. The types of incidents to be reported include criminal activity, accidents, vehicle accidents, medical emergencies, fire or safety emergencies, hazmat spills, reports of suspicious activity, and any other incident or activity in which any member of the security force becomes involved or believes is worth documenting. If in doubt, the security officer should complete an incident/complaint report.

Each incident/complaint report should be numbered, as an example, beginning with the year, the month, and numerical report number for the calendar year. For example, if the first incident of the year 2017 occurred on January 12, the report would be numbered as 01-12-2017-001; January 13, 2017, the date of the second report, would read 01-13-2017-002.

### Daily Activity Report

All security officers should complete a daily activity report during their shift. This report will be utilized to document their time of arrival and departure, inspection of the patrol vehicle, where applicable, and to document routine activities. Routine activities include building and door unlocking and locking, escorts, and checking of buildings in various areas of the cultural property. The daily activity report should also show the initial response to an incident or complaint, and reference the incident/complaint report number. The daily activity report should be maintained on file in the security office.

The security force training records need to be maintained by the chief security officer for all security staff and will be used to document the training of all security force members.

## Protection of Security Force Information

All information, whether received orally or in written form, pertaining to security force incidents or investigations being conducted is confidential information. Such information should only be disseminated to authorized individuals with a need to know. Information should not be released to individuals not associated with the cultural property unless approved by the chief security officer. Any requests for information from members of the media should be referred to the chief security officer.

All sensitive security documents must be secured in a locked security container when not being used. This includes both final and draft copies of incident reports, statements, investigative notes, safety and security reports, audits, and inspections. Sensitive documents that are no longer needed will be shredded prior to placing them in removal containers.

## Ethics and Conduct

All security force personnel are expected to maintain the highest professional and moral standards. The quality of a professional security force ultimately depends upon the willingness of the practitioners to observe special standards of conduct and to manifest good faith in professional relationships.

# Security Force Training

One of the most important aspects in the management of a security department is to ensure that the security officers are effectively trained to meet any state regulatory requirements as well as security industry standards of training. Such training will promote professionalism within the security force and reduce the liability risk. Security force training can be accomplished by on-the-job experience and training, and through the use of various formal education methods.

On-the-job experience and training is comprised of a structured and documented approach in instructing the new security officer with regard to their day-to-day duties. Each new security officer should be assigned to a mentor. The mentor may be a supervisor, lead officer, or training officer who will guide the new officer through their daily activities, providing instruction on how to perform their duties. As each new task is learned, it should be documented in a written training record for each security officer.

As the security officer accumulates time in the profession through various security assignments, they will gain knowledge and proficiency in their profession. Other on-the-job educational tools may include having the security officer take part in organizational meetings and committees to expand their professional knowledge. This may include being part of the security and safety committee or meetings related to special events that might be scheduled.

In addition to on-the-job training, more formal educational methods should also be applied. This may include company assistance for the security officer to obtain a college degree in security or criminal justice. In-service training can also be used, where the security officer is provided with information in a classroom environment covering security procedures, report writing, patrol methods, and court testament. In-service training can also be used to provide the security officer with various certifications, such as first aid and CPR, handcuff, OC, or baton certification.

Another option for education is to have the security officer take part in self-study by online proprietary training or a website offering free training such as the Department of Homeland Security Emergency Management Institute. Time for such online training can be provided during the work schedule or it can be accomplished off duty. Directed reading is another source of education where articles or documents related to security are made available in the security office in which the security officers are required to read and sign off on the document that it has been read.

In order to ensure that the security department is professionally trained, a security training program needs to be established and mandatory training needs to be provided to all security officers. All state regulatory training requirements, where applicable, must all be completed. It is important that all training completed by each security officer be documented in the security officer's training file. This will allow for the tracking of the training to ensure that it has been completed and such documentation is required by regulatory agencies or related to liability issues.

## Professional Security Certifications

Professional security certification can be obtained and is of value to those in the security profession. As previously discussed, ASIS International has developed several professional security certifications for individuals working in security supervision and management. ASIS also has two certifications for nonmanagement security professionals. The Professional Certified Investigator (PCI) was established for the security investigator or private investigator. Upon successful completion of the examination that covers all aspects of security and private investigation to include investigative methods, legal considerations, and interview methods, the designation of PCI is bestowed.

The Physical Security Professional (PSP) designation is designed for those in security who have responsibility for physical security within their institutional property such as a museum, historic site, archive, or library. The examination covers intrusion detection systems, barriers, security cameras, locks, and access control. Upon successful completion of the examination, the designation of Physical Security Professional (PSP) is bestowed.

Through the International Foundation for Protection Officers there is the Certified Protection Officer (CPO) designation. Upon successful completion of the examination, the designation is bestowed.

## Security Patrols

The primary duty of a security officer is to patrol the property. The purpose of the patrol function is to have the security officer at the right place at the right time to prevent losses due to criminal activity, safety concerns, and during an emergency. A uniformed security officer also is a deterrent and symbol of authority on the property.

Foot patrol is used to patrol inside of a structure and on property. It allows for close observation of the property and positive interaction with the property staff and visitors. In large structures, a small battery-operated security vehicle may be deployed for fast response, especially if there is a need to transport emergency equipment or individuals. Foot patrol is also utilized on the exterior of properties to patrol walkways, parking areas, and other segments of the property.

Properties with expansive parking areas, dock facilities, roadways, and open areas cannot be patrolled effectively on foot, especially during periods of cold and inclement weather. In these situations a means of patrol needs to be provided that will allow the security officer to cover large areas in a timely manner during both routine patrol and in response to service calls and emergencies. The most common means of patrol in this situation would be a motor vehicle assigned to the security department that is clearly marked as a security vehicle. It may be an all-wheel drive vehicle. This will be based on the roadways and layout of the property as well as the local climate. A property that is located in an area that receives snowfall should consider the use of an all-wheel drive security vehicle to ensure that security patrols can be accomplished in inclement weather or where there is a need for off-road capabilities.

During warm weather, bicycles may be considered as patrol vehicles. They allow for fast response and are a valuable public relations tool, as they promote more interaction with staff and visitors on the property.

To provide additional security at marinas and port facilities the security department may utilize small watercraft as security patrol boats to protect waterways, docks, yachts, and ships in the area (see Figure 7.7).

All security patrols must be conducted in a random manner so that patterns and predictability cannot be established. If the security patrol becomes predictable, then individuals with the intent of taking part in criminal activity to include industrial espionage be it property staff, professional criminals, or terrorists can plan their activity as not to be discovered by security patrols. If the security officer on patrol establishes patterns, then the officer can become complacent and less observant of their surroundings thus reducing the effectiveness of the security patrol. To reduce predictability, the security officer on patrol should use the concept of back tracking. An example of this would be if a security officer walks through an area, turns around, and walks back through the same area, or if the officer walks up a flight of stairs, turns around, and walks back down again.

There are two categories of patrol: supervised and unsupervised. Supervised patrol is one that is monitored and tracked by the use of proximity readers placed

**Figure 7.7 The author's previous 17-foot Boston Whaler. This type of watercraft is often used for security patrols around the dock areas of a marina or port. (Photograph by Daniel J. Benny.)**

throughout the museum, historic site, archive, or library structures and grounds that the security officer must activate as they make their set number of security rounds during their patrol schedule. This can also be accomplished by having the security officer communicate with the proprietary central station at set points during the patrol route.

The goal of this method is to document that the security did in fact cover all areas of the property and if monitored live to be alerted if the security office does not scan the reader. This provides safety for the officer in the event that there is a security incident taking place or the security has an accident or medical emergency. This method of supervised patrol is recommended when the security officer is conducting patrol during times when the cultural property is closed or when patrolling remote areas of the property.

During hours when the maritime property is open to the public, supervised patrol is not recommended. During those periods of time, the security officer should use unsupervised patrol meaning that the security officer does not need to check in at specified points on a patrol route. For the officers safety they should be required to check in by radio at predetermined time during their patrol schedule. The reason a supervised method of patrol is not recommended when the cultural property is open is that the security officer will be more concerned in documenting the supervised patrol that they may not be as effective in interacting with visitors and staff.

A security officer patrol awareness color code can be used to illustrate the proper attentiveness of a security officer during the course of their assigned shift.

■ White—This is when the security officer is unaware of their surroundings. The security officer is thinking of personal matters rather than being alert during patrol. A security, officers on patrol in the white awareness mode is not doing their job and is placing themselves, visitors, and staff at risk.

■ Green—This is the awareness color code for normal patrol. A security officer can and should be at this level of awareness during the entire patrol. In fact it is the level that everyone should be at when out and about in public places. At this level the security officer will use all of their senses. Vision is the number one sensor where the security officer can see all potential and actual threats. Hearing is the second most important sense. A security officer may hear an alarm going off, a call for help, or a transmission on the security radio. The security officer may also hear someone approaching in low visibility. Smell is also an important sensor in the security profession. A security officer may smell smoke or a natural gas leak and be able to prevent a serious incident. If a suspicious person approached the security officer and the person is intoxicated or has been smoking marijuana, the security officer may be able to smell it and be alert to an individual who may not be in their normal state of mind. The final sense is that of touch. This may be of value to the security officer to determine if equipment is overheating or if a vehicle found on the property was recently driven by the engine heat on the hood of the vehicle.

- Yellow—This is the level when the security officer is alert to something unusual based on one of the officer's senses. The security officer becomes alert and begins to evaluate the situation and makes a determination if it needs further investigation or return to normal patrol awareness or the green mode.
- Red—This is the full reaction mode where the security officer must respond to protect him- or herself, others, or the facility. If the security officer is alert, they should never be surprised and go from the green to the red mode. With that said, no one is perfect and it can happen.

It is critical that the security officer knows their patrol area. This means that the security officer should have a working knowledge of the physical layout of the site, including the interior of all buildings and the exterior property. The security officer needs to know what is normal based on the time of day and day of the week. This will allow them to discern what is not normal and alert them to suspicious criminal activity or a safety hazard. The security officer should also be aware of any special activity occurring during their patrol schedule such as special events, construction, or an area of the property that may be temporarily closed to the public.

When conducting the patrol the security officer should utilize the concepts of loss prevention and assets protection with the goal of prevention losses due to criminal activity and safety hazards. The patrol should be highly visible so that visitors and staff see the uniformed security officers frequently. This will also mean that any potential perpetrator will also see the security officers and it may deter unwanted activity.

## Apprehension and Arrest

Members of the security force are not police officers and generally will not make apprehensions and arrests. They should only act in accordance with the state law and company policy. Apprehensions and arrests may only be conducted should the security officer, where legal, witnesses the commission of a felony. Security officers may also make an apprehension of a violent person in order to protect themselves or another person from bodily harm.

## Bibliography

Fischer, R. J. and G. Green. *Introduction to Security.* 9th ed. Burlington, MA: Elsevier, 2012.
Kovacich, G. L. and E. P. Halibozek. *The Manager's Handbook for Corporate Security.* Burlington, MA: Elsevier, 2003.

## Chapter 8

# The Future of Private Investigation and Homeland Security

The future need for private investigators and the employment outlook of the private investigation profession in conducting traditional investigations as well as homeland security investigations are projected to grow by 5 percent from 2015 to 2024 (Figure 8.1). This is as fast as the average for all occupations. Technological advances have led to an increase in cybercrimes, such as identity theft, credit card fraud, and spamming. Internet scams, as well as other types of financial and insurance fraud, create demand for investigative services, particularly by the legal services industry. Background investigations will continue to be a source of work for many investigators, because both employers and personal contacts wish to verify a person's credibility. With the concerns related to international terrorism and protection of the homeland, private investigators will be needed to provide this service to private security in areas where the federal government security and intelligence service, and state and local law enforcement cannot.

Strong competition for jobs can be expected because the professional private investigation career attracts many qualified and educated individuals with extensive experience in law enforcement, the military, homeland security, and the intelligence community (Figure 8.1). The best job opportunities will be for entry-level positions in private investigation firms and for those who are qualified to become licensed and operate their own business. Those with extensive experience, college education, and professional certifications, as well as those with strong interviewing skills and familiarity with computers, will find more job opportunities than entry-level positions with investigative agencies.

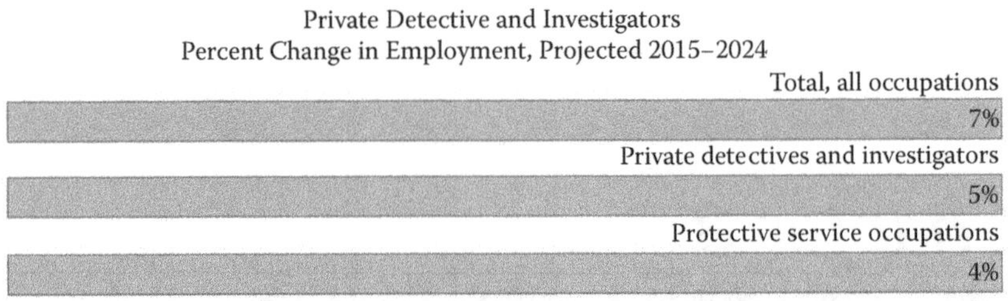

Private Detective and Investigators
Percent Change in Employment, Projected 2015–2024

Total, all occupations

7%

Private detectives and investigators

5%

Protective service occupations

4%

Note: "All occupations" includes all occupations in the U.S. economy.

**Figure 8.1  Outlook of private investigator positions. (From the U.S. Bureau of Labor Statistics, Employment Projections program.)**

Private investigators accounted for about 34,900 jobs in 2015. According to the U.S. Bureau of Labor Statistics, the industries that employed the most private detectives and investigators were as follows:

■ Investigations, guard and armored car services: 30 percent
■ Government: 7 percent
■ Finance and insurance: 6 percent
■ Commercial: 6 percent

# Investigative Technology

Every profession, vocation, and trade has its own specific tools and equipment to aid in the performance of its practitioners' assignments. The private investigation profession is no different. To be successful, it is essential that the private investigator has the correct equipment based on the assignment, be it case management, searching records, conducting surveillance, collecting and documenting evidence, or using physical security technology in protecting people and property.

The new investigative technology can be divvied into several generalized areas:

■ Administrative
■ Imagery
■ Electronic
■ Forensic
■ Transportation

## Administrative

Administrative technology includes innovative investigative software that can be used for case management, report writing, record keeping, budgeting, tax reporting, and inventory. There is also software that the private investigator can utilize to search online for public records, civil actions, criminal history, addresses, and social media.

## *Imagery*

Imagery includes the use of new digital still and video cameras and lenses that can be used for all situations. The traditional cameras are designed for surveillance for a distance with low-light capabilities, night vision, and zoom lenses. For close, covert surveillance the new miniature cameras and lenses facilitate their use in most any situation. Miniature cameras can be covertly hidden on the investigator as a body cam. They can also be hidden in common objects within a room so that they are undetectable. They can also be mounted on small, unmanned aerial vehicles for surveillance. When using such imagery equipment in the course of an investigation, it is important to have knowledge of the local, state, and federal laws related to imagery privacy issues so that such statutes are not violated.

## *Electronic*

Electronic equipment can allow the investigator, where permissible by law, to track individuals, vehicles, and property by use of GPS tracking systems. When using such electronic devices in the course of an investigation, it is important to have knowledge of the local, state, and federal laws related to electronic privacy issues so that such statutes are not violated by the private investigator.

# Investigative Certification, Education, and Training

The private investigative profession is more complex than ever and to meet the needs of their clients and provide homeland security, the private investigator must have a thorough understanding of current state-of-the-art investigative and security techniques and equipment. They must be well versed in both criminal and civil law and the rules of criminal procedure. Certified and educated practitioners in an occupational field such as private investigation also contribute to the attainment of professional stature, not only for that individual but also for all other investigators.

## *Professional Certification*

Attaining a professional certification is in itself an educational process. By holding a professional certification, the private investigator will be required to take part in continuing education in order to maintain the certification. Membership in professional organizations and subscriptions to professional investigative and homeland security journals also contribute to the private investigator's pool of knowledge (see Appendix C).

## College and University Education

The educational process should follow the private investigator throughout his or her entire career. The mere fact that one has a bachelor's degree in criminal justice, police administration, security administration, or homeland security is not an indication that their educational experience is over; it is never over. To keep abreast of the constant changes within the profession, higher degrees and continuing education is vital.

There are many sources of education, including formal college and university degree programs in the classroom or online. Continuing education programs offered by colleges and universities are also of value to the private investigator. Seminars and workshops offered by professional organizations, private vendors, and governmental agencies such as the U.S. Department of Homeland Security can keep the private investigator current in their profession.

There are colleges and universities throughout the United States and globally that offer degree programs including doctorate, master's, bachelor's, and associate's degrees in areas of security administration, homeland security, criminal justice, and police administration. Some institutions offer 30-credit certificates in these topic areas that are related and advantageous to the private investigation professional. Many colleges and universities offer noncredit continuing education courses, workshops, and seminars on investigative and homeland security topics.

## Educational Resources Available through Professional Organizations

Taking an active part in professional organizations can be educationally beneficial because it provides opportunities for networking with other professional members as well as participation in annual seminars and workshops. Most professional organizations publish journals, books, and audiovisual educational material. Some organizations sponsor professional certification programs, which attaining is an educational experience in itself (see Appendix B).

# Bibliography

Fischer, R. J. and G. Green. *Introduction to Security.* 9th ed. Burlington, MA: Elsevier, 2012.
Kovacich, G. L. and E. P. Halibozek. *The Manager's Handbook for Corporate Security.* Burlington, MA: Elsevier, 2003.

# Appendix A: State Licensing for Private Investigators

- Alabama—http://revenue.alabama.gov/index.cfm
- Alaska—http://www.labor.state.ak.us/research/dlo/fprvdet.htm
- Arizona—http://licensing.azdps.gov/Licenseprivateinvestigator.asp
- Arkansas—http://www.asp.state.ar.us/
- California—http://www.bsis.ca.gov/
- Colorado—https://www.colorado.gov/dora/boards_programs
- Connecticut—http://www.ct.gov/despp/site/default.asp
- Delaware—http://dsp.delaware.gov/
- Florida—http://www.freshfromflorida.com/Divisions-Offices/Licensing
- Georgia—http://sos.ga.gov/index.php/licensing/plb/42/faq
- Hawaii—http://cca.hawaii.gov/
- Idaho—http://legislature.idaho.gov/legislation/1998/H0770.html
- Illinois—http://ilga.gov/legislation/ilcs/ilcs4.asp?DocName=0225044
  70HArt.+15&ActID=2474&ChapterID=24&SeqStart=1700000&Seq
  End=2200000
- Indiana—http://www.in.gov/pla/pisg.htm
- Iowa—http://www.dps.state.ia.us/asd/pi_licensing.shtml
- Kansas—https://www.accesskansas.org/kbi/pi_verify/helpfulhints.html
- Kentucky—http://kpi.ky.gov/Pages/default.aspx
- Louisiana—http://lsbpie.com/
- Maine—http://legislature.maine.gov/legis/statutes/32/title32sec8105.html
- Maryland—http://misahq.com/wordpress2/
- Massachusetts—http://www.mass.gov/eopss/law-enforce-and-cj/law
  -enforce/prof-stds/cert-unit/pi-license-requirements.html
- Michigan—http://www.michigan.gov/lara/0,4601,7-154-61343_35414
  _60647_35469---,00.html
- Minnesota—https://dps.mn.gov/Pages/default.aspx

- Mississippi—http://www.mpia.org/
- Missouri—http://pr.mo.gov/pi.asp
- Montana—http://bsd.dli.mt.gov/license/bsd_boards/psp_board/board _page.asp
- Nebraska—http://www.sos.ne.gov/licensing/private_eye/index.html
- Nevada—http://www.leg.state.nv.us/NAC/NAC-648.html
- New Hampshire—http://www.nh.gov/safety/divisions/nhsp/
- New Jersey—http://www.njsp.org/private-detective/private-detective-rules.shtml
- New Mexico—http://www.rld.state.nm.us/boards/Private_Investigations _Requirements_and_Continuing_Education.aspx
- New York—http://www.dos.ny.gov/licensing/
- North Carolina—http://www.ncapi.com/index.php?option=com_content&view =article&id=82&Itemid=85
- North Dakota—http://www.nd.gov/pisb/index.html
- Ohio—http://codes.ohio.gov/oac/4501:5-1
- Oklahoma—http://oklegal.onenet.net/oklegal-cgi/get_statute?98 /Title.59/59-1750.2.html
- Oregon—http://www.oregon.gov/DPSST/PS/pages/howtoapplypi.aspx
- Pennsylvania—http://www.pali.org/
- Rhode Island—http://webserver.rilin.state.ri.us/Statutes/TITLE5/5-5/INDEX .HTM
- South Carolina—http://www.sled.sc.gov/
- South Dakota—http://dci.sd.gov/LawEnforcementTraining/FrequentlyAsked Questions.aspx
- Tennessee—http://sos.tn.gov/
- Texas—http://www.txdps.state.tx.us/rsd/psb//
- Utah—http://www.rules.utah.gov/publicat/code/r722/r722-330.htm
- Vermont—https://www.sec.state.vt.us/professional-regulation.aspx
- Virginia—http://www.dcjs.virginia.gov/pss/index.cfm
- Washington—http://www.dol.wa.gov/business/pi/
- Washington, DC—http://mpdc.dc.gov/page/security-officers-management -branch-somb
- West Virginia—http://www.sos.wv.gov/business-licensing/licensing/pages /applyingforanindividualpilicense.aspx
- Wisconsin—http://dsps.wi.gov/Licenses-Permits/PrivateDetective
- Wyoming—http://wyomingdci.wyo.gov/dci-operations-section/pi-faqs

# Appendix B: Professional International and National Private Investigative and Intelligence Organizations and Publications

Private professional intelligence organizations and associations are an excellent source of information related to private investigation and homeland security. Through such organizations' web pages, magazines, journals, and newsletters, valuable information can be obtained. Organizations also provide investigative, intelligence, and homeland security training, seminars, workshops, and professional certifications. Memberships in these organizations are also an excellent source for networking and exchanging valuable security and counterespionage information.

## Association of Former Intelligence Officers

The Association of Former Intelligence Officers was founded in 1975. The original name was the Association of Retired Intelligence Officers. The name change was made in order to represent all of the members, retired and active. The change also expanded the pool of eligible members. As a member of the intelligence community, the Association of Former Intelligence Officers' mission is to educate the public about the intelligence community and to conduct intelligence-related training and research.

Association of Former Intelligence Officers
6723 Whittier Avenue, Suite 200
McLean, VA 22101-4533
Telephone: 703-790-0320
E-mail: afio@afio.com
Web page: http://www.afio.com

# Business Espionage Controls and Countermeasures Association

The Business Espionage Controls & Countermeasures Association (BECCA) was founded in 1986 by Dr. William M. Johnson as an informal group of industrial espionage professionals and experts. The mission of BECCA is to provide information, training, and a certification program for counterespionage professionals. Johnson publishes the BECCA newsletter, *The Business Espionage Report.*

BECCA was incorporated on June 22, 1990, as the Business Espionage Controls & Countermeasures Association (BECCA), a nonprofit organization in Washington State.

> The purpose of the association is to research and exchange information about business espionage controls and countermeasures; to establish and encourage a code of ethics within the profession, and to promote our professional image within the business community through a Certified Confidentiality Officer (CCO) Program. It is organized exclusively for, and will be operated for scientific, literary, and educational purposes. The Certified Confidentiality Officer Program is approved by the DOD, the Higher Education Coordinating Board of Washington State, and the Department of Veterans Affairs.

BECCA
PO Box 55582
Shoreline, WA 98155-0582
Web page: http://www.becca-online.org/
E-mail: Office@BECCA-onine.org

# International Association for Intelligence Education

In June 2004, the International Association for Intelligence Education (IAFIE) was founded after a gathering of intelligence studies of professional trainers and college educators. The group was formed from innumerable intelligence disciplines such as national security, public law enforcement, and competitive and corporate intelligence, for the purpose of having a professional association that could provide a vehicle to share information within the intelligence studies profession globally.

As stated on its web page, the organization's purpose is "Expanding research, knowledge, and professional development in intelligence education; Providing a forum for the exchange of ideas and information for those interested in and concerned with intelligence education; Advancing the intelligence profession by setting standards, building resources, and sharing knowledge in intelligence studies."

The organization also builds relationships and cultivates professional communication among professionals in the intelligence community and academia, business, and governmental agencies.

International Association for Intelligence Education
PO Box 10508
Erie, PA 16514
Telephone: 814-824-2131
Web page: http://www.iafie.org/

# International Spy Museum

The International Spy Museum is the only public museum in the United States that is solely dedicated to espionage. The museum provides a global viewpoint on the history of intelligence, its role in society, and national security in the past and present.

The International Spy Museum has the largest collection of espionage artifacts from around the world to be exhibited at one location. The mission of the International Spy Museum is the education of the public about the intelligence profession and industrial espionage.

The museum concentration is on human intelligence and the part spies have played in world events throughout history. The museum presents the information in an apolitical method to give an overview of the history of espionage.

International Spy Museum
800 F Street, NW
Washington, DC 20004
Telephone: 202-EYE-SPYU (202-393-7798)
E-mail: membership@spymuseum.org
Web page: http://www.spymuseum.org/visit/

## Naval Intelligence Professionals

Founded in 1985 as a nonprofit organization, the goal of the Naval Intelligence Professionals (NIP) is to further the knowledge of the maritime intelligence profession, and to provide an exchange of information so that present and former Naval Intelligence professionals may be kept informed of current developments in the Naval Intelligence community. NIP is established as a nonprofit organization incorporated to enhance awareness of the mission and vital functions of the Naval Intelligence community.

It is a professional intelligence association of current active duty, reserve, and retired officers, as well as enlisted and Department of Navy civilians who serve or have served within the Naval Intelligence community.

Naval Intelligence Professionals
PO Box 11579
Burke, VA 22009-1579
E-mail: navintpro@aol.com
Web page: http://navintpro.net/

## ASIS International

ASIS International is the foremost society for security professionals internationally. Founded in 1955 as the American Society for Industrial Security, it is devoted to security professionals by providing professional publications and educational programs. This includes the ASIS Annual Seminar and Exhibits. ASIS International also publishes the industry's number one magazine *Security Management.*

ASIS administers three internationally accredited certification programs. The Certified Protection Professional (CPP) board certification in security management is the highest professional certification one can achieve in the security profession. It is recognized globally. Two specialty certifications are also administered: the Professional Certified Investigator (PCI) and the Physical Security Professional (PSP).

ASIS International
1625 Prince Street
Alexandria, VA 22314
Telephone: 702-519-6200
E-mail: asis@asisonline.org
Web page: http://www.asisonline.org

## American Board for Certification in Homeland Security

The American Board for Certification in Homeland Security (ABCHS) encompasses a membership of active and retired military, law enforcement, and security professionals. The ABCHS membership includes the globe's leading homeland security professionals. The ABCHS is committed to providing education, research, and professional certification to the homeland profession. This is accomplished through publications, conferences, and professional certifications.

American Board for Certification in Homeland Security
2750 East Sunshine Street
Springfield, MO 65804
1-877-219-2519
Web page: http://www.abchs.com/about/

## Association of British Investigators

Formed in 1913, the Association of British Investigators (ABI) has been upholding professional standards in England for over a century. It is the most important private investigative organization in the United Kingdom with members from around the world.

Association of British Investigators
95/297 Church Street
Blackpool, Lancashire FY1 3PJ
England
Telephone: 012532975
E-mail: info@theaib.org.uk
Web page: http://www.theabi.org.uk

## Association of Certified Fraud Examiners

The Association of Certified Fraud Examiners (ACFE) is the world's largest and most professional anti-fraud organization. It is the "premier provider of anti-fraud training and education. With nearly 65,000 members, the ACFE is reducing business fraud world-wide and inspiring public confidence in the integrity and objectivity within the profession."

The Certified Fraud Examiner (CFE) credential can be earned through the organization and documents one's proven expertise in fraud prevention, detection, and deterrence. CFEs around the world help protect the global economy and homeland security by preventing and uncovering fraud.

Association of Certified Fraud Examiners
The Gregor Building
716 West Avenue
Austin, TX 78701-2727
Telephone: 800-245-3321
E-mail: memberservices@acfe.com
Web page: http://www.acfe.com/

## Council of International Investigators

The Council of International Investigators (CII) is a professional private investigative organization. It offers professional networking and the Certified International Investigator designation. This designation is awarded if the applicant qualifies as a licensed private investigator and is a full member of the organization. The organization also publishes the newsletter *The Councilor*.

Council of International Investigators
PO Box 563
Elmhurst, IL 60126
Telephone: 630-501-1880
Web page: http://www.cii2.org/

## National Association of Legal Investigators

The National Association of Legal Investigators (NALI) is a professional investigative organization that exemplifies the legal investigator who works solely for law firms and the legal profession. NALI offers the Certified Legal Investigator designation based on experience and passing a qualification exam. The organization publishes the journal *The Legal Investigator*.

NALI World Headquarters
235 N. Pine Street
Lansing, MI 48933
Telephone: 1-866-520-NALI (6254)
Web page: http://nalionline.org/

## National Council of Investigation and Security Services

The objective of the National Council of Investigation and Security Services is to "monitor national legislative and regulatory activities affecting the investigation and security industry." Much of the council's activities are to assist, advise, inform, and influence legislation. The organization works to encourage the practice of high standards of personal and ethical conduct of those in the private investigation profession and contract security profession.

National Council of Investigation and Security Services
7501 Sparrows Point Blvd.
Baltimore, MD 21219-1927
Telephone: 800-445-8408
E-mail: inquire@nciss.org
Web page: www.nciss.org

## World Association of Detectives

The World Association of Detectives current name was adopted in 1966. The organization was founded in 1925 as the World Secret Service Association. The World Association of Detectives provides a professional publication and annual international conferences and workshops around the globe. The World Association of Detectives is the number one private investigative professional organization in the world.

World Association of Detectives
7501 Sparrows Point Blvd.
Baltimore, MD 21219-1927
Telephone: 443-982-4585
E-mail: wad1924@comcast.net
Web page: www.wad.net

## PI Magazine

*PI Magazine* is an independent private investigative publication.

PI Magazine
870 Pompton Avenue, Suite B2
Cedar Grove, NJ 07009
Telephone: 973-571-0400
Web page: www.pimagazine.com

# Appendix C: Professional Private Investigation Certifications

## ASIS International

ASIS International is the largest professional security organization on the globe. It offers the Certified Protection Professional (CPP) for those private investigators in management positions as a professional security designation. For nonmanagement, it offers the Professional Certified Investigator (PCI) designation.

ASIS International
1625 Prince Street
Alexandria, VA 22314-2818
Telephone: 703-519-6200
Web page: www.asisonline.org

## National Association of Legal Investigators

The National Association of Legal Investigators established in 1973 the Certified Legal Investigator (CLI) designation in order to provide a certification to investigators who work for the legal profession.

National Association of Legal Investigators
908 21st Street
Sacramento, CA 95814-3118
Telephone: 916-441-5522
Web page: www.nalionline.org

# Appendix D: Private Investigative Agency Contract Security Force Checklist

The following list provides a guideline of issues to consider if the private investigative firm provides a contract security service to clients. The items on the list that should be considered are based on the contract and mission of the security force.

- Does the investigative firm contract out security officers?
  - Security guard service?
  - Patrol service?
- Does the location employ a chief/director of security or site manager?
  - Identify the chief/director.
  - Provide a copy of the director's resume or employment application.
  - If no director of security, who is responsible for maintaining security at the location?
- How many security officers are assigned to each shift at a contract location?
  - Uniformed?
  - Plainclothes?
- Is there a security supervisor for each shift?
  - Security director?
  - Assistant director of security?
  - Captain?
  - Lieutenant?
  - Sergeant?
  - Senior security officer?
- Weapons
  - Firearms

- Baton (straight or PR-24)
- Chemical agents (tear gas or Mace)
- If armed, do the security officers have lawful certification indicating that they passed the proper courses and possess valid authorization to carry said weapons?
■ Training
  - Are the security officers trained in first aid?
  - Are the security officers trained in fire control and prevention?
  - Are the security officers trained in the legal aspects of apprehension and detention?
  - What other training is provided to the security officers?
■ Do the security officers wear uniforms?
  - Badges?
  - Sleeve patches?
  - Type of shirt and trousers.
  - Hats?
■ Do security officers patrol the premises?
  - Indicate patrol routes.
  - Provide times of patrols.
  - Specific duties during patrols.
■ Do security officers stand (or sit) at stationary posts?
  - Identify post locations.
  - What are the security officers' duties at said posts?
  - Are there written "post orders" at every location where security officers are stationed?
■ Do security officers drive patrol vehicles?
  - Are the patrol vehicles marked, identifying them as "security?"
  - Do the vehicles have special lights or flashing beacons?
  - Are the vehicles equipped with two-way radios?
  - List any other emergency equipment on or in patrol vehicles.
■ Are security officers required to maintain daily activity logs?
  - Obtain copies of the logs during the day of the incident and for one week prior.
  - Are the security officers required to write reports or fill out specific incident report forms?
  - Does the security department or any other department of the company file reports and logs, and/or maintain an index file or computerized record of said reports?
  - Who reviews the logs and reports?
■ What are the security officers' rate of pay, beginning with the entry-level salary?
■ What procedures are used to verify security officer applications (e.g., check former employer, education, training)?
  - What other preemployment background investigations are conducted?

# Appendix E: Pennsylvania Private Detective Act

The applicable law concerning licensed private detectives in the Commonwealth of Pennsylvania is the Private Detective Act of 1953, as amended, and is outlined in the Pennsylvania Statutes Annotated, Title 22. The act was originally passed on August 21, 1953 (P.L. 1273, No. 361).

## The Private Detective Act of 1953, as Amended

§ 11. Short Title
§ 12. Definitions
§ 13. Licenses
§ 14. Application for Licenses
§ 15. Enforcement of Act; Investigations
§ 16. Issuance of Licenses; Fees; Bonds
§ 17. Refund of Fees
§ 18. Posting and Surrender of License Certificates
§ 19. Certificate, Pocket Card, or Badge Lost or Destroyed
§ 20. Removal of Bureau, Agency, or Office
§ 21. Renewal of Licenses
§ 22. License Certificates, Pocket Cards, Shields, or Badges
§ 23. Employees
§ 24. Employees Not to Divulge Information or Make False Reports
§ 25. Application of Act
§ 26. Unlawful Acts
    § 26.1 Penalty for Unlicensed Acts
§ 27. District Attorneys to Prosecute
§ 28. Reward May Be Presumed
§ 29. Roster of Licenses
§ 30. Disposition of Fees and Other Revenue

## § 11. Short Title

This act shall be known and may be cited as "The Private Detective Act of 1953."

## § 12. Definitions

a. "Private detective business" shall mean and include the business of private detective, private detective business, the business of investigator, or the business of watch, guard, or patrol agency.
b. "Private detective business" shall also mean and include, separately or collectively, the making for hire, reward, or for any consideration whatsoever, of any investigation or investigations for the purpose of obtaining information with reference to any of the following matters, notwithstanding the fact that other functions and services may also be performed for fee, hire, or reward:
   1. Crimes or wrongs done or threatened against the government of the United States of America or any state or territory of the United States of America.
   2. The identity, habits, conduct, movements, whereabouts, affiliations, associations, transactions, reputation, or character, of any person, group of persons, association, organization, society, other groups of persons, partnership, or corporation.
   3. The credibility of witnesses or other persons.
   4. The whereabouts of missing persons.
   5. The location or recovery of lost or stolen property.
   6. The causes and origin of, or responsibility for, fires, or libels, or losses, or accidents, or damage, or injuries, to real or personal property.
   7. The affiliation, connection, or relation, of any person, partnership, or corporation, with any union, organization, society, or association, or with any official member or representative thereof.
   8. With references to any person or persons seeking employment in the place of any person or persons who have quit work by reason of any strike.
   9. With reference to the conduct, honesty, efficiency, loyalty, or activities, of employees, agents, contractors, and subcontractors.
   10. The securing of evidence to be used before any authorized investigating committee, board of award, board of arbitration, or in the trial of civil or criminal cases.
   11. The furnishing, for hire or reward, of watchmen, or guards, or private patrolmen, or other persons, to protect persons or property, or to prevent the theft or the unlawful taking of goods, wares, and merchandise, or to prevent the misappropriation or concealment of goods, wares, or merchandise, money, bonds, stocks, in action, notes, or other valuable documents, papers, and articles of value, or to procure the return thereof, or the performing of the service of such guard or other person, or any of said purposes.

The forgoing shall not be deemed to include persons engaged in the business of investigators for or adjusters for insurance companies, nor persons in the exclusive employment of common carries subject to regulation by the interstate commerce commission or the Public Utility Commission of the Commonwealth of Pennsylvania, nor any telephone, telegraph or other telecommunications company subject to regulation by the Federal Communications Commission or the Public Utility Commission of the Commonwealth of Pennsylvania or an employee of any such company while performing any investigatory activities engaged in by his employer, or investigators in the employment of credit bureaus.

c. The terms "the business of detective agency," the "business of investigator," the "business of watch, guard, or patrol agency"; and the terms "private detective" or "investigator" shall mean and include any person, partnership, association, or corporation, engaged in the private detective business, as defined in subsections (a) and (b) of this section, with or without the assistance of any employee or employees.

d. The term "commissioner" shall mean the Commissioner of the Pennsylvania State Police.

e. The term "patrol agency" shall mean and include any agency and/or individuals (including therein security guards, uniformed or non-uniformed) employed full time or part time, on a temporary or permanent basis, who, for any consideration whatsoever, patrols, guards, protects, monitors, regulates, secures, or watches over persons and/or property, either real or personal. This term specifically includes any person employed in any capacity, for any length of time, to protect property, either real or personal, against labor strikes or against any person or persons who have become a party to any labor strike.

## § 13. Licenses

a. No person, partnership, association, or corporation, shall engage in the business of private detective, or the business of investigator, or the business of watch, guard, or patrol agency, for the purpose of furnishing guards or patrolmen or other persons to protect persons or property, or to prevent the theft of the unlawful taking of goods, wares, and merchandise, or to prevent the misappropriation or concealment of goods, wares, or merchandise, money, bonds, stocks, documents, and other articles of value, for hire or reward, or advertise his or their business to be that of detective, or of a detective agency, or investigator, or watch, guard, or patrol agency, notwithstanding the mane or title used in describing such agency, or notwithstanding the fact that other functions and services may also be performed for fee, hire, or reward, without having first obtained a license so to do as hereinafter provided.

b. No person, partnership, association, or corporation, shall engage in the business of furnishing or supplying for fee, hire, or any consideration or reward, information as to the personal character or activities of any person, partner-ship, corporation, society, or association, or any person or group of persons, or as to the character or kind of the business and occupation of any person, partnership, corporation, society, or association or any person or group of persons, or as to the character or kind of the business and occupation of any person, partnership, or corporation, or own or conduct or maintain a bureau or agency for the above mentioned purposes, except exclusively as to the financial rating, standing, and credit responsibility of persons, partner-ships, associations, or corporations, or as to the personal habits and financial responsibility of applicants for insurance, indemnity bonds, or commercial credit, or of claimants under insurance policies: Provided, That the business so exempted does not embrace other activities described in subsections (a), (b), and (c) of section two of this act (*§ 12 of this title—Definitions*) without having first obtained, as hereafter provided, a license to do so, for each such bureau or agency, and for each and every subagency, office, and branch office to owned, conducted, managed, or maintained by such persons, partnership, association, or corporation, for the conduct of said business.

c. Nothing contained in this section shall be deemed to include the busi-ness of investigators for or adjusters for insurance companies, nor persons in the exclusive employment of common carries subject to regulation by the interstate commerce commission or the Public Utility Commission of the Commonwealth of Pennsylvania, nor any telephone, telegraph, or other telecommunications company subject to regulation by the Federal Communications Commission or the Public Utility Commission of the Commonwealth of Pennsylvania or an employee of any such company while performing any investigatory activities engaged in by his employer, or inves-tigators in the employment of credit bureaus.

## § 14. Application for Licenses

Any person, partnership, association or corporation, intending to conduct a private detective business, the business of investigator, or the business of watch, guard, or patrol agency, or the business of a detective agency, and any person, partnership, association, or corporation, intending to conduct the business of furnishing or sup-plying information as the personal character of any person, partnership, corpora-tion, society, or association or any person or group of persons, or intending to own, conduct, manage, or maintain a bureau or agency for the above mentioned pur-poses, or, while engaged in other lawful business activities, also intending to engage in any one or more of the activities set forth in subsections (a), (b), and (c) of section two of this act (*§ 12 of this title—Definitions*), except exclusively as to the financial rating, standing, and credit responsibility of persons, partnerships, associations, or corporations, shall, for each such bureau or agency, and for each and every sub-agency, office and branch office to be owned, conducted, managed or maintained by such person, partnership, association, or corporation for the conduct of such business, file, in the office of the clerk of the court of common pleas of the county wherein the principal office or such business is located, a written application, duly signed and verified, as follows:

a. If the applicant is a person, the application shall be signed and verified by such person, and if the applicant is a partnership or association, the application shall be signed and verified by each individual composing or intending to compose such partnership or association. The application shall state the full name, age, residence, present and previous occupations, of each person or individual so signing the same, that he is a citizen of the United States, and shall also specify the name of the city, borough, township, or incorporated town, stating the street and number if the premises have a street and number, and otherwise such apt description as will reasonably indicate the location thereof, where is to be located the principal place of business, and the bureau, agency, subagency, office or branch office for which the license is desired, and such further facts as may be required by the court of common pleas, to show the good character, competency, and integrity of each person or individual so signing such application. Each person or individual signing such application shall, together with such application, submit to the court of common pleas his photograph, in duplicate, in passport size, and also fingerprints of his two hands, recorded in such manner as may be specified by the court of common pleas. Before approving such application, it shall be the duty of the court of common pleas to compare such fingerprints with fingerprints of criminals now or hereafter filed in the records of the Pennsylvania State Police. Every such applicant shall establish, to the satisfaction of the court of common pleas and by at least two duly acknowledged certificates, that such applicant, if he be a person, or, in the case of a partnership, association, or corporation, at least one member of such partnership, association, or corporation, has been regularly employed as a detective, or shall have been a member of the United States government investigative service, a sheriff, a member of the Pennsylvania State Police, or a member of a city police department of a rank or grade higher than that of patrolman, for a period of not less than three years. Such application shall be approved as to each person or individual so signing the same by not less than five reputable citizens of the community in which such applicant resides or transacts business, or in which it is proposed to own, conduct, manage, or maintain the bureau, agency, subagency, office, or branch office for which the license is desired, each of whom shall certify that he has personally known the said person or individual for a period of at least five years prior to the filing of such application, that he has read such application and believes each of the statements made therein to be true, that such person is honest, of good character, and competent, and not related or connected to the person so certifying by blood or marriage.

The certificate of approval shall be signed by such reputable citizens and duly verified and acknowledged by them before an officer authorized to take oaths and acknowledgment of deeds.

b. If the applicant is a corporation, the application shall be signed and verified by the president, secretary and treasurer thereof, and shall specify the name of the corporation, the date and place of its incorporation, the location of its principal place of business, and the name of the city, borough, township, or incorporated town, stating the street and number if the premises have a street and number, and otherwise such apt description as will reasonably indicate the location thereof, where is to be located the principal place of business, and the bureau, agency, subagency, office or branch office for which the license is desired, the amount of the corporation's outstanding paid up capital stock and whether paid in cash or property, and, if in property, the nature of the same, and shall be accompanied by a duly certified copy of its certificate of incorporation. Each and every requirement of clause (a) of this section as to a person or individual member of a partnership or association shall apply to the president, secretary, and treasurer, and each such officer, his successor and successors, shall, prior to entering upon the discharge of his duties, sign and verify a like statement, approved in like manner, as is by clause (a) prescribed in the case of a person or individual member of a partnership or association. In the event of the death, resignation, or removal of such officer, due notice of that fact shall forthwith be given in writing to the court of common pleas, together with a copy of the minutes of any meeting of the board of directors of said corporation, certified by the secretary, indicating the death, resignation, or removal of such officer, and the election or designation of the successor of such deceased, resigned, or removed officer.

## § 15. Enforcement of Act; Investigations

a. The district attorneys of the various counties shall have the power to enforce the provisions of this act, and upon complaint of any person, or on his own initiative, to investigate any violation thereof, or to investigate the business, business practices, and business methods of any person, partnership, association or corporation applying for or holding a license as a private detective or investigator if, in the opinion of the district attorney, such investigation is warranted. Each such applicant or licensee shall be obliged, on request of the district attorney, to supply such information as may be required concerning his or its business, business practices, or business methods, or proposed business practices or methods.

b. For the purpose of enforcing the provisions of this act and in making investigations relating to any violation thereof, and for the purpose of investigating the character, competency, and integrity of the applicants or licensees hereunder, and for the purpose of investigating the business, business practices, and business methods of any applicant or licensee, or of the officers or agents thereof, the district attorney, acting by such officer or person in the office of the district attorney as the district attorney may designate, shall have the power to subpoena and bring before the officer or person so designated any person in the county, and require the production of any books or papers which he deems relevant to the inquiry, and administer an oath to, and take testimony of, any person, or cause his deposition to be taken, with the same fees and mileage and in the same manner as prescribed by law for civil cases in a court of record, except that any applicant, or licensee, or officer, or agent thereof, shall not be entitled to such fees or mileage. Any person duly sub-poenaed who fails to obey such subpoena with reasonable cause, or without such cause refuses to be examined or to answer any legal or pertinent question as to the character or qualification of such applicant or licensee or such applicant's or licensee's business, business practices, and methods, or such violations, shall be guilty of a misdemeanor, and upon conviction thereof, shall be sentenced to pay a fine of not more than five hundred dollars ($500) or to undergo imprisonment for not more than one (1) year, or both. The testimony of witnesses in any such proceeding shall be under oath, which the district attorney or his subordinate designated by the district attorney may administer, and willful, false swearing in any such proceeding shall be punishable as perjury.

## § 16. Issuance of Licenses; Fees; Bonds

a. When the application shall have been examined, and such further inquiry and investigation made as the court of common pleas or the district attorney shall deem proper, and when the court of common pleas shall be satisfied there from of the good character, competency, and integrity of such appli-cant, or, if the applicant be a partnership, association, or corporation, of the individual members or officers thereof, and a period of ten days from the date of the filing of the application shall have passed, the court of common pleas shall issue and deliver to such applicant a certificate of license to conduct such business, and to own, conduct, or maintain a bureau, agency, subagency, office, or branch office for the conduct of such business on the premises stated in such application, upon the applicant's paying to the court of common pleas for each such certificate of license so issued, for the use of the county, a license fee of two hundred dollars ($200), if the applicant be an individual, or of three hundred dollars ($300), if a partnership, association, or corporation, and upon the applicant's executing, delivering, and filing in the office of the clerk of the court of common pleas a corporate bond in the sum of ten thou-sand dollars ($10,000), conditioned for the faithful and honest conduct of such business by such applicant, which surety bond must be written by a cor-porate surety company authorized to do business in this Commonwealth as surety, and approved by the court of common pleas with respect to its form, manner of execution, and sufficiency. The license granted pursuant to this act shall last for a period of two years, but shall be revocable at all times by the court of common pleas for cause shown. In the event of such revocation or of a surrender of such license, no refund shall be made in respect of any license fee paid under the provisions of this act. Such bond shall be executed to the Commonwealth of Pennsylvania, and any person injured by the violation of any of the provisions of this act, or by the willful, malicious, and wrongful act of the principal or employee, may bring an action against such principal, employee, or both, on said bond, in his own name, to recover damages suffered by reason of such willful, malicious, and wrongful act: Provided, That the aggregate liability of the surety for all such damages shall in no event exceed the sum of such bond. In each and every suit of prosecution arising out of this act, the agency of any employee as to the employment and as to acting in the course of his employment shall be presumed.

The license certificate shall be in a form to be prescribed by the court of common pleas, and shall specify the full name of the applicant, the location of the principal office or place of business, and the location of the bureau, agency, subagency, office, or branch office for which the license is issued, the date on which it is issued, the date on which it will expire, and the names and residences of the applicant or applicants filing the statement required by section four (*§ 14 of this title—Application for Licenses*) upon which the license is issued, and in the event of a change of any such address or residence, the court of common pleas shall be duly notified in writing of such change within twenty-four hours thereafter, and failure to give such notification shall be sufficient cause for revocation of such license. No such license shall be issued to a person under the age of twenty-five years.

b. Except as hereinafter provided in this subsection, no such license shall be issued to any person who has been convicted in this State or any other state or territory of a felony, or any of the following offenses: (1) illegally using, carrying, or possessing a pistol or other dangerous weapon; (2) making or possessing burglar's instruments; (3) buying or receiving stolen property; (4) unlawful entry of a building; (5) aiding escape from prison; (6) unlawfully possessing or distributing habit forming narcotic drugs; (7) picking pockets or attempting to do so; (8) soliciting any person to commit sodomy or other lewdness; (9) recklessly endangering another person; (10) making terroristic threats; or (11) committing simple assault.

Except as hereinafter in this subsection provided, no license shall be issued to any person whose license has been previously revoked by the court of common pleas or the authorities of any other state or territory because of conviction of any of the crimes or offenses specified in this section. The provisions of this subsection shall not prevent the issuance of a license to any person who, subsequent to his conviction, shall have received executive pardon therefore removing this disability.

c. There shall be kept in the office of the clerk of the court of common pleas a bulletin board, in a place accessible to the general public, on which shall be posted, at noon on Friday of each week, the following: a statement of all pending applications for licenses under this act, giving the name of the applicant, and whether individual, partnership, association, or corporation, and the proposed business address, a similar statement of all such licenses issued during the preceding week, a similar statement of all such licenses revoked during the preceding week.

d. No holder of an employment agency license shall be licensed under this act. While holding a license under this act, a licensee shall not, simultaneously, hold an employment agency license, or have financial interest in, or participate in the control and management of, any employment agency, or any other person, partnership, association, or corporation engaged in private detective business, except that a licensee hereunder may own or possess stock in any corporation whose only business is to undertake, for hire, the preparation of payrolls and the transportation of payrolls, moneys, securities, and other valuables, or whose only business is to provide or furnish protective or guard service to the government of the United States, or any subdivision, department, or agency of the government of the United States. In the event of the filing in the office of the clerk of the court of common pleas a verified statement of the objection to the issuance of a license under the provisions of this act, no license shall be issued to such applicant until all objections shall have been heard in a hearing and a determination made by the court of common pleas.

## § 17. Refund of Fees

Moneys heretofore or hereafter received by the court of common pleas pursuant to this act may, within three years from the receipt thereof, be refunded to the person entitled thereto on satisfactory proof that:

1. Such moneys were in excess of the amount required by this act, to the extent of such excess.
2. The license for which application was made has been denied.
3. The applicant for the license has predeceased its issuance.
4. The licensee has enlisted in or been otherwise inducted into active Federal military, naval, or marine service, or in any branch or division thereof, in which event the refund shall be such proportion of the license fee paid as the number of full months remaining unexpired of the license period bears to the total number of the months in such period.

Such refunds shall, upon approval by the court of common pleas, be paid from any moneys received from the operation of this act and in the custody of the county treasures.

## § 18. Posting and Surrender of License Certificate

Immediately upon receipt of the license certificate issued by the court of common pleas pursuant to this act, the licensee named therein shall cause such license certificate to be posted up and at all times displayed in a conspicuous place in the bureau, agency, subagency, office, or branch office for which it is issued, so that all persons visiting such place may readily see the same. Such license certificate shall, at all reasonable times, be subject to inspection by the district attorney or an authorized representative or representatives of the Pennsylvania State Police and the Attorney General. It shall be unlawful for any person, partnership, association, or corporation holding such license certificate to post such certificate, or to permit such certificate to be posted, upon premises other than those described therein, or to which it has been transferred pursuant to the provision of this act, or knowingly to alter, deface, or destroy any such license certificate. Every license certificate shall be surrendered to the court of common pleas within seventy-two hours after its term shall have expired, or after notice in writing to the holder that such license has been revoked. Any licensee failing to comply with any of the provisions of this section shall be guilty of a misdemeanor, and, upon conviction thereof, shall be sentenced to pay a fine of not more that five hundred dollars ($500) or to undergo imprisonment for not more than (1) year, or both. Such failure shall be sufficient cause for the revocation of a license.

## § 19. Certificate, Pocket Card, or Badge Lost or Destroyed

If it shall be established to the satisfaction of the court of common pleas, in accordance with rules and regulations promulgated and established by such court, that an unexpired license certificate, pocket card, or badge issued in accordance with the provisions of this act has been lost or destroyed without fault on the part of the holder, the court of common pleas shall issue a duplicate license certificate or pocket card for the unexpired portion of the term of the original license certificate, and shall issue a duplicate badge for the unexpired portion of the term of the original license, upon payment to the court of common pleas of an amount required for such duplicate badge.

## § 20. Removal of Bureau, Agency, or Office

If the holder of an unexpired license certificate issued pursuant to this act shall remove the bureau, agency, subagency, office, or branch office to a place other than that described in the license certificate, he shall, within the twenty-four hours immediately following such removal, give written notice of such removal to the court of common pleas. Such notice shall describe the premises to which such removal is made, and the date on which it was made. Such license certificate shall be sent to the court of common pleas. A judge of such court shall cause to be written or stamped across the face of such license certificate a statement signed by him to the effect that the holder of such license has removed, on the date stated in such written notice, such bureau, agency, subagency, office, or branch office from the place originally described in such license certificate to the place described in such written notice, and such license certificate, with the endorsement thereon, shall then be returned to the licensee named therein.

## § 21. Renewal of Licenses

a. A license granted under the provisions of this act may be renewed by the clerk of courts upon application therefor by the holder thereof upon payment of fee and filing of surety bond, each in amounts equivalent to those specified in section 6 (*§ 16 of this title—Issuance of Licenses; Fees; Bonds*) as pertaining to original licenses.

b. A brief renewal application form shall be prescribed by the Attorney General. Fingerprints and references shall not be required with a renewal application. The clerk of courts shall reissue the license for a period of up to five years, without a mandatory waiting period, unless the clerk perceives a problem, which requires submission of the renewal application to the court.

c. A renewal period, with the meaning of this act, is considered as being six months from the date of expiration of a previously issued license.

## § 22. License Certificates, Pocket Cards, Shields, or Badges

Upon the issuing of a license as hereinbefore provided, the court of common pleas shall issue to each such person, individual member of a partnership or association, or officer of a corporation making and filing a statement required by section 4 of this act (*§ 14 of this title—Application for Licenses*), a pocket card, of such size and design as such court may prescribe, which card shall contain a photograph of the licensee, the name and business address of the licensee, and the imprint or impress of the seal of the court, and also a metal shield or badge, of such shape and description and bearing such inscription as the court may designate, which pocket card and badge shall be evidence of due authorization pursuant to the terms of this act. All persons to whom such license certificates, pocket cards, shields, or badges shall have been issued shall be responsible for the safe keeping of the same, and shall not loan, let, or allow any other person to use, wear, or display such certificate, pocket card, shield, or badge. No person shall wear or display any license certificate, pocket card, shield, or badge, purporting to authorize the holder or wearer thereof to act as a private detective or investigator, unless the same shall have been duly issued pursuant to the provisions of this act. Failure to comply with the provisions of this section shall be sufficient cause for revocation of such license, and all such certificates, pocket cards, shields, and badges shall be returned to the court of common pleas within seventy-two hours after the holder thereof has received notice in writing of the expiration or revocation of such license. No person, except as authorized in this section, shall wear or display a shield or badge of any design or material, purporting to indicate that the wearer or bearer thereof is a private detective or investigator or is authorized to act as a private detective or investigator, unless required by law to do so. Any person violating the provisions of this section shall be guilty of a misdemeanor, and upon conviction thereof, shall be sentenced to pay a fine of not more than five hundred dollars ($500) or to undergo imprisonment for not more than one (1) year, or both.

## § 23. Employees

a. The holder of any license certificate issued pursuant to this act may employ to assist him in his work of private detective or investigator as described in section 2 (*§ 12 of this title—Definitions*) and in the conduct of such business as many persons as he may deem necessary, and shall at all times during such employment be legally responsible for the good conduct in the business of each and every person so employed and shall be responsible for the reasonable supervision of said employees' conduct.

No holder of any unexpired license certificate issued pursuant to this act shall knowingly employ in connection with his or its business, in any capacity whatsoever, any person who has been convicted of a felony, or any of the following offenses, and who has not, subsequent to such conviction, received executive pardon therefor removing this disability: (1) illegally using, carrying or possessing a pistol or other dangerous weapon; (2) making or possessing burglar's instruments; (3) buying or receiving stolen property; (4) unlawful entry of a building; (5) aiding escape from prison; (6) unlawfully possessing or distributing habit forming narcotic drugs; (7) picking pockets or attempting to do so; (8) soliciting any person to commit sodomy or other lewdness; (9) any person whose private detective or investigator's license was revoked or application for such license was denied by the court of common pleas or by the authorities of any other state or territory because of conviction of any of the crimes or offenses specified in this section; (10) recklessly endangering another person; (11) terroristic threats; or (12) committing simple assault.

A holder of an unexpired license certificate issued pursuant to this act who knowingly employs a person who has been convicted of a felony or any of the offenses specified in this section shall be guilty of a misdemeanor and, upon conviction thereof, shall be sentenced to pay a fine of not more than five thousand dollars ($5000) or to undergo imprisonment for not more than one (1) year, or both.

A first conviction for violation of this section may subject the license holder to revocation of his license by the issuing authority.

Upon the second conviction of a license holder for knowingly hiring a person convicted of a felony or other specified offenses in this section, the license of said holder shall be revoked.

Should the holder of an unexpired license certificate falsely state or represent that a person is or has been in his employ, such false statement or misrepresentation shall be sufficient cause for the revocation of such license. Any person falsely stating or representing that he is or has been a detective or employed by a detective agency shall be guilty of a misdemeanor, and, upon conviction thereof, shall be sentenced to pay a fine of not more than five hundred dollars ($500) or to undergo imprisonment for not more than one (1) year, or both.

b. No person shall hereafter be employed by any holder of a license certificate until he shall have executed and furnished to such license certificate holder a verified statement to be known as "employee's statement," setting forth:

1. His full name, age, and residence address;
2. The country of which he is a citizen;
3. The business or occupation engaged in for the three years immediately preceding the date of the filing of the statement setting forth the place or places where such business or occupation was engaged in, and the name or names of employers, if any;
4. That he has not been convicted of a felony, or of any offense involving moral turpitude, or of any of the misdemeanors or offenses described in subsection (a) of this section;
5. That he holds current and valid certification under the act of October 10, 1974 (P.L. 705, No. 235), known as the "Lethal Weapons Training Act," if, as an incidence to employment, he will carry a lethal weapon.
6. Such further information as the court of common pleas may by rule require to show the good character, competency, and integrity of the person executing the statement.

c. The license holder shall act with due diligence in that the necessary steps to ensure the veracity of the employee's statement, and immediately upon the verification of an employee's statement, the holder of a license certificate by whom such person has been or is to be employed shall cause two sets of fingerprints of the two hands of such person to be recorded in such manner as the court of common pleas may by rule prescribe. The holder of a license certificate shall immediately stamp, in indelible ink, the employee's statement and each set of fingerprints with the name, year, and license certificate number of such holder, and a number, which number shall be determined by the number of such statements furnished to such holder and shall be in numerical sequence.

d. The holder of a license certificate shall affix one set of such fingerprints to the employee's statement, in such manner that the prints can be examined without disclosing the contents of the employee's statement, and shall retain such statement and prints so long as he shall be licensed under this act.

e. The holder of a license certificate shall file the other set of fingerprints with the court of common pleas. Proof of the employee's current and valid certification under the "Lethal Weapons Training Act" must also be submitted to the court if the employee will carry a lethal weapon as an incidence to employment.

f. Within five days after the filing of such fingerprints, the court of common pleas shall cause such fingerprints to be compared with fingerprints of criminals now or hereafter filed in the records of the Pennsylvania State Police, and if the court finds any record affecting such prints, it shall immediately notify the holder of such license certificate and shall also refer the matter to the district attorney of the county. The common pleas court may also, from time to time, cause such fingerprints to be checked against the fingerprints of criminals now or hereafter filed in the records of the Pennsylvania State Police or of other official fingerprint files within or without this Commonwealth, and if the court finds that such person has been convicted of a felony or any other offense specified in subsection (a) of this section, he shall immediately notify the holder of such license certificate and shall also refer the matter to the district attorney. The common pleas court shall at all times be given access to and may from time to time examine the fingerprints retained by the holder of a license certificate as provided in subsection (d) of this section.

g. If any holder of a certificate shall file with the common pleas court the fingerprints of a person other than the person so employed, he shall be subject to a fine not exceeding five thousand dollars ($5000) or to imprisonment not exceeding one (1) year, or both.

## § 24. Employees Not to Divulge Information or Make False Reports

Any person who is or has been an employee of a holder of a license shall not divulge to any one other than his employer or as his employer shall direct, except as he may be required by law, any information acquired by him during such employment in respect of any of the work to which he shall have been assigned by such employer. Any such employee violating the provisions of this section, and any such employee who shall willfully make a false report to his employer in respect of any of such work, shall be guilty of a misdemeanor, and, upon conviction thereof, shall be sentenced to pay a fine of not more than five hundred dollars ($500) or to undergo imprisonment for not more than one (1) year, or both. The employer of any employee believed to have violated this section shall, without any liability whatsoever upon said employer, supply the court of common pleas, and such court shall, should the facts and circumstances be deemed to warrant, conduct further investigation and submit the evidence thus acquired to the district attorney for appropriate action in accordance with the provision of section 18 of this act (*§ 28 of this title—Reward May Be Presumed*).

## § 25. Application of Act

Nothing in this act shall apply to any detective officer or man belonging to the Pennsylvania State Police, or to the police force of any county, city, borough, township, or incorporated town, or any employee of such State Police, or such police force, appointed or elected by due authority of law, while engaged in the performance of their official duties, nor to any person, partnership, association, or corporation or any bureau or agency, whose business is exclusively the furnishing of information as to the business and financial standing and credit responsibility of persons, partnerships, associations, or corporations, or as to the personal habits and financial responsibility of applicants for insurance, indemnity bonds, or commercial credit, or of any claimants under insurance policies, and whose business does not embrace other activities described in section 2 of this act (*§ 12 of this title— Definitions*), nor to any corporation duly authorized by the Commonwealth to operate a fire alarm protection business, or to any person while engaged in the business of adjuster for an insurance company, nor to any person regularly employed as special agent, detective, or investigator exclusively by one employer in connection with the affairs of that employer only, nor to any charitable or philanthropic society or association duly incorporated under the laws of the Commonwealth and which is organized and maintained for the public good and not for private profit, nor shall anything in this act contained be construed to affect in any way attorneys or counselors at law in the regular practice of their profession, but such exemption shall not enure to the benefit of any employee or representative of such attorney or counselor at law who is not employed solely, exclusively, and regularly by such attorney or counselor at law, nor to persons in the exclusive employment of common carriers subject to regulation by the interstate commerce commission or the Public Utility Commission of the Commonwealth of Pennsylvania, nor any telephone, telegraph, or other telecommunications company subject to regulation by the Federal Communications Commission or the Public Utility Commission of the Commonwealth of Pennsylvania or an employee of any such company while performing any investigatory activities engaged in by his employer, or investigators in the employment of credit bureaus. No person, partnership, association corporation, or any bureau or agency, exempted hereunder from the application of this act, shall perform any manner of detective service as described in section 2 (*§ 12 of this title—Definitions*) hereof for any other person, partnership, association, corporation, bureau, or agency, whether for fee, hire, reward, other compensation, remuneration, or consideration, or as an accommodation without fee, reward, or remuneration, or by a reciprocal arrangement whereby such services are exchanged on request of parties thereto. The commission of a single act prohibited by this act shall constitute a violation thereof.

Nothing in this act shall be construed to affect or prohibit the right of any person to form, or become affiliated with, or to continue as a member of, any union, association, society, or organization of his own choosing.

## § 26. Unlawful Acts

It is unlawful for the holder of a license issued under this act, or for any employee of such licensee, knowingly to commit any of the following acts, within or without the Commonwealth of Pennsylvania: to incite, encourage, or aid in the incitement or encouragement of, any person or persons who have become a party to any strike to do unlawful acts against the person or property of any one, or to incite, stir up, create, or aid in the inciting of discontent or dissatisfaction among the employees of any person, partnership, association, or corporation with the intention of having them strike, to interfere or prevent lawful and peaceful picketing during strikes, to interfere with, restrain, or coerce employees in the exercise of their right to form, join, or assist any labor organization of their own choosing, to interfere or hinder the lawful or peaceful collective bargaining between employees and employers, to pay, offer, or give any money, gratuity, favor, consideration, or other thing of value, directly or indirectly, to any person, for any verbal or written report of the lawful activities of employees in the exercise of their right of self-organization, to form, join, or assist labor organizations, and to bargain collectively through representatives of their own choosing, to advertise for, recruit, furnish, or replace, or offer to furnish or replace, for hire or reward, within or without the Commonwealth of Pennsylvania, any help or labor, skilled or unskilled, or to furnish or offer to furnish armed guards, other than armed guards theretofore regularly employed, for the protection of payrolls, property, or premises, for service upon property which is being operated in anticipation of or during the course or existence of a strike, or furnish armed guards upon the highways for persons involved in labor disputes, or to furnish or offer to furnish to employers or their agents, any arms, munitions, tear gas, implements, or any other weapons, or to send letters or literature to employers offering to eliminate labor unions, or distribute or circulate any list of members of a labor organization, or to advise any person of the membership of an individual in a labor organization for the express purpose of preventing those so listed or named from obtaining or retaining employment. The violation of any of the provisions of this section shall constitute a misdemeanor, and, upon conviction thereof, shall be punishable by a fine of not less than five hundred dollars ($500) nor more than five thousand dollars ($5000), or to imprisonment for not less than six (6) months nor more than (1) year, or both. If the holder of a license shall violate any of the provisions in this section, the license holder may be subject to the revocation of his license by the issuing authority. Upon the second conviction of a license holder for violation of any of the provisions in this section, the license of said holder shall be revoked.

## § 26.1 Penalty for Unlicensed Acts

Any person in violation of the provision of section 3(a) (*§ 13 of this title—Licenses*) by reason of engaging in the private detective business without a license, shall upon conviction thereof, be guilty of a misdemeanor of the third degree.

## § 27. District Attorneys to Prosecute

Criminal action for violation of this act shall be prosecuted by the district attorney of the county in which any violation of this act occurred.

## § 28. Reward May Be Presumed

In any prosecution under this act, any person, partnership, association, or corporation, who or which performs or commits any of the acts set forth in sections 2 and 3 (*§ 12 of this title—Definitions and § 13 of this title—Licenses*), shall be presumed to do so for a fee, compensation, valuable consideration, or reward.

## § 29. Roster of Licenses

The clerk of each court of common pleas shall publish, at least once in each year, a roster of the names and addresses of all persons, partnerships, associations, and corporations licensed by such court under the provisions of this act. A copy of each roster published by each clerk shall be mailed by him to any licensee upon request and without charge, and a copy of each such roster shall also be mailed by him to the commissioner, who shall keep a roster of the names and addresses of all persons, partnerships, associations and corporations in the Commonwealth of Pennsylvania under the provisions of this act. A copy of the roster kept by the commissioner shall be mailed by him to any licensee upon request and without charge.

## § 30. Disposition of Fees and Other Revenue

All fees and other money derived from the operation of this act shall, on the first day of each month, be paid by the court of common pleas into the county treasury.

# Appendix F: Pennsylvania Lethal Weapons Training Act

## Lethal Weapons Training Act

## Act of Oct. 10, 1974, P.L. 705, No. 235

## Cl. 22

### An Act

Providing for the training and licensing of watch guards, protective patrolmen, detectives and criminal investigators, carrying and using lethal weapons in their employment; imposing powers and duties on the Commissioner of the Pennsylvania State Police; and providing penalties.

### Table of Contents

The General Assembly of the Commonwealth of Pennsylvania hereby enacts as follows:

Section 1. Short Title—This act shall be known and may be cited as the "Lethal Weapons Training Act."

Section 2. Legislative Findings and Purpose—(a) The General Assembly finds that there are private detectives, investigators, watchmen, security guards and patrolmen, privately employed within this Commonwealth who carry and use lethal weapons including firearms as an incidence of their employment and that there have been various tragic incidents involving these individuals which occurred because of unfamiliarity with the handling of weapons. The General Assembly also finds that there is presently no training required for such privately employed agents in the handling of lethal weapons or in the knowledge of law enforcement and the protection of rights of citizens, and that such training would be beneficial to the safety of the citizens of this Commonwealth.

(b) It is the purpose of this act to provide for the education, training and certification of such privately employed agents who, as an incidence to their employment, carry lethal weapons through a program administered or approved by the Commissioner of the Pennsylvania State Police.

Section 3. Definitions—As used in this act:

"Commissioner" means the Commissioner of the Pennsylvania State Police.

"Full-time police officer" means any employee of a city, borough, town, township or county police department assigned to law enforcement duties who works a minimum of two hundred days per year. The term does not include persons employed to check parking meters or to perform only administrative duties, nor does it include auxiliary and fire police. (Def. added Feb. 20, 1982, P.L.88, No.32)

"Lethal weapons" include but are not limited to firearms and other weapons calculated to produce death or serious bodily harm. A concealed billy club is a lethal weapon. The chemical mace or any similar substance shall not be considered as "lethal weapons" for the purposes of this act. (Def. amended Nov. 23, 1976, P.L.1155, No.254)

"Privately employed agents" include any person employed for the purpose of providing watch guard, protective patrol, detective or criminal investigative services either for another for a fee or for his employer. Privately employed agents do not include local, State or Federal Government employees or those police officers commissioned by the Governor under the act of February 27, 1865 (P.L.225, No.228). The term shall include a police officer of a municipal authority. (Def. amended Dec. 14, 1982, P.L.1209, No.278)

"Program" means the education and training program established and administered or approved by the commissioner in accordance with this act.

Section 4. Education and Training Program—(a) An education and training program in the handling of lethal weapons, law enforcement and protection of rights of citizens shall be established and administered or approved by the commissioner in accordance with the provisions of this act.

(b) All privately employed agents, except those who have been granted a waiver from compliance herewith by the commissioner who, as an incidence to their employment, carry a lethal weapon shall be required to attend the program established by subsection (a) of this section in accordance with the requirements or regulations established by the commissioner and, upon satisfactory completion of such program, shall be entitled to certification by the commissioner. ((b) amended Nov. 23, 1976, P.L.1155, No.254)

(c) Except for colleges and universities, no nongovernment employer of a privately employed agent who, as an incidence to his employment, carries a lethal weapon, shall own, operate, or otherwise participate in, directly or indirectly, the establishment or administration of the program established by subsection (a) of this section.

Section 5. Power and Duties of Commissioner—The commissioner shall have the power and duty:

1. To implement and administer or approve the minimum courses of study and training for the program in the handling of lethal weapons, law enforcement and protection of the rights of citizens.
2. To implement and administer or approve physical and psychological testing and screening of the candidate for the purpose of barring from the program those not physically or mentally fit to handle lethal weapons. However, candidates who are full-time police officers and have successfully completed a physical and psychological examination as a prerequisite to employment or to continued employment by their local police departments or who have been continuously employed as full-time police officers since June 18, 1974 shall not be required to undergo any physical or psychological testing and screening procedures so implemented. ((2) amended Feb. 20, 1982, P.L.88, No.32)
3. To issue certificates of approval to schools approved by the commissioner and to withdraw certificates of approval from those schools disapproved by the commissioner.
4. To certify instructors pursuant to the minimum qualifications established by the commissioner.
5. To consult and cooperate with universities, colleges, community colleges and institutes for the development of specialized courses in handling lethal weapons, law enforcement and protection of the rights of citizens.
6. To consult and cooperate with departments and agencies of this Commonwealth and other states and the Federal Government concerned with similar training.

7. To certify those individuals who have satisfactorily completed basic educational and training requirements as established by the commissioner and to issue appropriate certificates to such persons.
8. To visit and inspect approved schools at least once a year.
9. In the event that the commissioner implements and administers a program, to collect reasonable charges from the students enrolled therein to pay for the costs of the program.
10. To make such rules and regulations and to perform such other duties as may be reasonably necessary or appropriate to implement the education and training program.
11. To grant waivers from compliance with the provisions of this act applicable to privately employed agents who have completed a course of instruction in a training program approved by the commissioner. ((11) added Nov. 23, 1976, P.L.1155, No.254)

Section 6. Certificate of Qualification—(a) Any person desiring to enroll in such program shall make application to the commissioner, on a form to be prescribed by the commissioner.

(b) The application shall be signed and verified by the applicant. It shall include his full name, age, residence, present and previous occupations and such other information that may be required by the commissioner to show the good character, competency and integrity of the applicant.

(c) The application shall be personally presented by the applicant at an office of the Pennsylvania State Police where his fingerprints shall be affixed thereto. The application shall be accompanied by two current photographs of the applicant of a size and nature to be prescribed by the commissioner and a thirty-five dollar ($35) application fee, unless the applicant is a full-time police officer, in which case no application fee shall be required. Thereafter the application shall be forwarded to the commissioner. ((c) amended Feb. 20, 1982, P.L.88, No.32)

(d) The fingerprints of the applicant shall be examined by the Pennsylvania State Police and the Federal Bureau of Investigation to determine if he has been convicted of or has pleaded guilty or nolo contendere to a crime of violence. The commissioner shall have the power to waive the requirement of Federal Bureau of Investigation examination. Any fee charged by the Federal agency shall be paid by the applicant. ((d) amended Dec. 14, 1982, P.L.1209, No.278)

(e) No application shall be accepted if the applicant is under the age of eighteen.

(f) After the application has been processed and if the commissioner determines that the applicant is eighteen years of age and has not been convicted of or has not pleaded guilty or nolo contendere to a crime of violence, and has satisfied any other requirements prescribed by him under his powers and duties pursuant to section 5, he shall issue a certificate of qualification which shall entitle the applicant to enroll in an approved program.

**Compiler's Note:** Section 6(a) of Act 48 of 1981, which provided for the fixing of fees charged by administrative agencies, provided that section 6(c) is repealed insofar as it establishes a set fee for any activity inconsistent with the fees set forth in Act 48.

Section 7. Certification and Fee—(a) A certification fee of not more than fifteen dollars ($15) shall be paid by each individual satisfactorily completing the program prior to the receipt of a certificate.

(b) The commissioner shall furnish to each individual satisfactorily completing the program, an appropriate wallet or billfold size copy of the certificate, which shall include a photograph of the individual thereon.

(c) Every certified individual shall carry his wallet or billfold size certificate on his person as identification during the time when he is on duty or going to and from duty and carrying a lethal weapon.

(d) Certification shall be for a period of five years.

(e) Privately employed agents who, as an incidence to their employment, carry a lethal weapon shall be required to renew their certification within six months prior to the expiration of their certificate. The commissioner shall prescribe the manner in which the certification shall be renewed, and may charge a nominal renewal fee therefore, not to exceed fifteen dollars ($15).

**Compiler's Note:** Section 6(a) of Act 48 of 1981, which provided for the fixing of fees charged by administrative agencies, provided that section 7(a) is repealed insofar as it establishes a set fee for any activity inconsistent with the fees set forth in Act 48.

Section 8. Good Standing—(a) Privately employed agents must possess a valid certificate whenever on duty or going to and from duty and carrying a lethal weapon.

(b) Whenever an employer of a privately employed agent subject to the provisions of this act discharges him for cause, the employer shall notify the commissioner of such within five days of the discharge.

(c) The commissioner may revoke and invalidate any certificate issued to a privately employed agent under this act whenever he learns that false, fraudulent or misstated information appears on the original or renewal application or whenever he learns of a change of circumstances that would render an employee ineligible for original certification.

Section 8.1. Retired Police Officer—(a) A nondisability retired police officer of a Pennsylvania municipality or the Pennsylvania State Police shall be initially certified under this act, and need not meet the training and qualification standards or physical and psychological qualifications hereunder, if he was a full-time police officer for at least twenty years, retired in good standing and has assumed the duties of a privately employed agent on or before three years from the date of his retirement.

If a retired police officer commences his duties as a privately employed agent after three years from the date of his retirement he must meet the physical and psychological requirements of this act for certification under this section.

(b) A retired police officer initially certified under this section shall not be required to pay the application fee but shall pay the certification fee upon the submission of a completed application provided by the commissioner. (8.1 added Dec. 14, 1982, P.L.1209, No.278)

Section 9. Penalties—(a) Any privately employed agent who in the course of his employ carries a lethal weapon, and who fails to comply with subsection (b) of section 4 or with subsection (a) of section 8 of this act, shall be guilty of a misdemeanor and upon conviction shall be subject to imprisonment of not more than one year or payment of a fine not exceeding one thousand dollars ($1000), or both.

(b) Any privately employed agent who in the course of his employ carries a lethal weapon, and who violates subsection (c) of section 7 of this act shall be guilty of a summary offense, and, upon conviction, shall pay a fine not exceeding fifty dollars ($50).

Section 10. Prohibited Act—No individual certified under this act shall carry an inoperative or model firearm while employed and he shall carry only a powder actuated firearm approved by the commissioner.

Section 10.1. Active Police Officers—All active police officers subject to the training provisions of the act of June 18, 1974 (P.L.359, No.120), referred to as the Municipal Police Education and Training Law, shall be granted a waiver of the training requirements of this act upon presentation to the commissioner of evidence of their completion of the training requirements of the Municipal Police Education and Training Law and the successful completion of a biennial firearms qualification examination administered by their respective police agency. (10.1 added Apr. 4, 1990, P.L.112, No.26)

Section 11. Effective Date—Sections 1, 2, 3, subsections (a), (b), and (c) of section 4, sections 5, 6, 7, subsections (a), (b), and (c) of section 8, and sections 9 and 10 of this act shall take effect December 31, 1975. (11 amended July 25, 1975, P.L.101, No.52)

# Appendix G: Virginia Private Investigator Training Course Outline

## Commonwealth of Virginia

## Private Investigator

## Training Course Outline

Private Investigator (02E)—60 hours (excluding examination and practical exercises)

- a. Orientation
    1. Applicable sections of the Code of Virginia
    2. 6VAC20-171, Regulations Relating to Private Security Services
    3. Standards of professional conduct
    4. Ethics
    5. Signs of terrorism
- b. Law—One Practical Exercise
    1. Basic law
    2. Legal procedures and due process
    3. Criminal and civil law
    4. Evidence
    5. Legal privacy requirements
- c. General Investigative Skills—One Practical Exercise
    1. Tools and techniques
    2. Surveillance
    3. Research
    4. Interviewing
- d. Documentation—One Practical Exercise
    1. Report preparations
    2. Photography

3. Audio recording
4. General communication
5. Courtroom testimony
e. Types of Investigations—One Practical Exercise
1. Accident
2. Insurance
3. Background
4. Domestic
5. Undercover
6. Fraud and financial
7. Missing persons and property
8. Criminal

Written comprehensive examination.

# Appendix H: New York Security Guard Training

## New York State Security Guard Training Requirements

Section 89-G of Article 7A requires all persons engaged in security guard activities be registered with the New York Department of State (DOS), and complete all training (unless exempt) at schools approved by the Division of Criminal Justice Services (DCJS). The following training courses are required.

## Security Guard (Unarmed)

### Initial Training Requirements

**8 Hour Pre-Assignment Training**—A general introductory course. You must complete this course and submit a copy of the certificate issued to you with your security guard application.

**16 Hour On-the-Job Training (OJT)**—A course relevant to the duties of guards, requirements of the work site, and the needs of the employer. You must complete this training within 90 days of employment as a security guard.

### Annual Training Requirement

**8 Hour Annual In-Service Training**—This course must be completed each calendar year you hold a security guard registration. Your registration is issued for two years, therefore, you must complete two 8 Hour Annual In-Service training courses within your registration effective and expiration dates to be eligible for renewal.

# Armed Security Guard

## *Initial Training Requirements*

**8 Hour Pre-Assignment Training**—A general introductory course. You must complete this course and submit a copy of the certificate issued to you with your security guard application.

**16 Hour On-the-Job Training (OJT)**—A course relevant to the duties of guards, requirements of the work site, and the needs of the employer. You must complete this training within 90 days of employment as a security guard.

**47 Hour Firearms Training**—You must possess a valid NYS Pistol Permit and security guard registration to enroll in this course. Upon successful completion of this course, submit a copy of the certificate with your application for an armed guard registration upgrade.

## *Annual Training Requirements*

**8 Hour Annual In-Service Training**—This course must be completed each calendar year you hold an armed security guard registration. Your registration is issued for two years, therefore, you must complete two 8 Hour Annual In-Service training courses within your registration effective and expiration dates to be eligible for renewal; and

**8 Hour Annual Firearms Training**—This course must also be completed each calendar year you hold an armed security guard registration. Your registration is issued for two years, therefore, you must complete two 8 Hour Annual Firearms training courses within your registration effective and expiration dates to be eligible for renewal.

**Peace Officer Waivers**—Applications for a waiver of firearms training for unarmed and armed security guards may be reviewed up to a maximum of four years after separation from a non-exempt, sworn, full-time peace officer position in New York. *If you are a separated police officer or exempt peace officer, do not submit a waiver application, see exemptions below.* For the purposes of registration, you may be granted a waiver from training if you can demonstrate completion of training that meets or exceeds the minimum standards for the 8 Hour Pre-Assignment, OJT, or 47 Hour Firearms courses. To request a waiver, call DCJS directly at (518) 457-6726, or contact them in writing at 80 South Swan Street, 3rd floor, Albany NY 12210-8002. If approved, DCJS will send you a waiver letter to submit with your security guard application to DOS.

# Exemptions (Do Not Require a Waiver from DCJS)

## *I. Police Officers*

The Security Guard Act *exempts **active** police officers* from the definition of a security guard. This means active police officers accepting secondary employment are *not* required to register or complete training. However, if you are an active police officer, anticipating retirement, and still wish to obtain a Security Guard Registration, you must provide proof of original police officer training and a letter of good standing from the agency that employs you, along with the original Security Guard Application and finger print receipt.

### *Retired Police Officers*

In order to be exempt from the training, you must provide DOS with a letter from your department (signed by your department) indicating your retirement date. In addition, if you are required by your security guard employer to carry a firearm, or are authorized to have access to a firearm, you must provide proof to DOS and your employer of having completed a Basic Course for Police Officers (or an equivalent course), that included initial firearms training, within one year prior to employment as an armed security guard.

If your initial firearms training occurred more than a year before employment as an armed security guard, you must complete an 8 Hour Annual Firearms Course for Security Guards and report that training to DOS and your employer.

- ■ If it has been more than 10 years since you retired as a police officer, you are additionally required to complete the 8 Hour Annual In-Service Training Course for Security Guards every year thereafter.

## *II. Peace Officers*

Section 170.1 of Title 19 NYCRR exempts from the definition of a security guard, any individual designated as a peace officer under Article 2 of the NYS Criminal Procedure Law (CPL). The powers of a peace officer are only valid while the individual is acting in his or her official capacity for their primary employer. Consequently, during outside employment (moonlighting), a peace officer is no longer acting in his or her official capacity, and, therefore, must register and complete all training, (unless the individual has either been *waived*, or is *exempt* [based on specific job titles] (see *Recent Amendments that may have a direct affect on you*, below).

## Current Peace Officers Applying for Firearms Training Waivers

If your employer has authorized you to carry a firearm in the line of duty, and you have been employed for 18 months or more and can exhibit a valid certificate, you are exempt from the 47 Hour Firearms Course, and the addition 8 Hour Annual Firearms Course for holders of an armed security guard registration. Individuals seeking registration as an armed guard, must provide the Department of State with a copy of a waiver letter (issued by DCJS) and a certificate of completion for the MPTC Basic Course for Peace Officers with Firearms, or both the Basic Course for Peace Officers without Firearms and Firearms and Deadly Physical Force [long firearms course].

## Recent Amendments That May Have a Direct Effect on You

Section 89-n (4) GBL has been amended to exempt certain categories of peace officers (see *Categories of Peace Officers Exempt from Training per Amendment to §89-n (4) GBL*, below) from the following training: 47 Hour Firearms Course, 8-Hour Pre-Assignment, OJT, and 8 Hour Annual In-Service. To qualify for an exemption, a peace officer must either be currently employed in one of the job titles (see *Categories of Peace Officers Exempt from Training per Amendment to §89-n (4) GBL*, below), or retired from one of those job titles for *not* more than 10 years. Although exempt from the 8 Hour Annual In-Service training course for the first 10 years of retirement, the retired peace officer is subject to an 8 Hour Annual Firearms training course, if their basic course was completed more than a year prior to filing their security guard application.

**Note:** If it has been more than 10 years since an individual retired as a peace officer, they are required to completed the 8 Hour Annual In-Service Training Course for Security Guards, and additionally, if armed, the 8 Hour Annual In-Service Firearms Training Course every year thereafter.

## Categories of Peace Officers Exempt from Training per Amendment to §89-n (4) GBL

A. *Sheriffs, Undersheriffs, and Deputy Sheriffs of NYC, and sworn officers of the Westchester County Department of Public Safety Services as defined in NYS CPL, §2.10 (2):* In order to be exempt from the 47 Hour Firearms Training Course, 8-Hour Pre-Assignment, OJT, and Annual In-Service Training, individuals must provide the Department of State with either a copy of their Basic Course for Peace Officers certificate, or a letter from the personnel office of the entity for which they work(ed), indicating basic peace officer training. If currently employed, they must also provide a copy of their ID card showing current employment in one of the appropriate law enforcement categories, and that they are in good standing.

B. *Security Personnel for the Triborough Bridge and Tunnel Authority as defined in NYS CPL, §2.10 (20):* In order to be exempt from the 47 Hour Firearms Training Course, 8-Hour Pre-Assignment, OJT, and Annual In-Service Training, individuals must provide the Department of State with either a copy of their Basic Course for Peace Officers certificate, or a letter from the personnel office of the entity for which they work(ed), indicating basic peace officer training. If currently employed, they must also provide a copy of their ID card showing current employment in one of the appropriate law enforcement categories, and that they are in good standing.

C. *Uniformed Court Officer as defined in NYS CPL, §2.10 (21) (a):* In order to be exempt from the 47 Hour Firearms Training Course, 8-Hour Pre-Assignment, OJT, and Annual In-Service Training, individuals must provide the Department of State with either a copy of their Basic Course for Peace Officers certificate, or a letter from the academy indicating their academy training. These courses must meet or exceed the MPTC basic course without firearms. In addition, if the individual is in an armed position, the individual must have completed MPTC Basic Course for Peace Officer with Firearms, or both the Basic Course for Peace Officers without Firearms and Firearms and Deadly Physical Force [long firearms course]. If currently employed, the individual must also provide a copy of their ID card showing current employment, and that they are in good standing.

D. *Court Clerks as defined in NYS CPL, §2.10 (21) (b):* In order to be exempt from the 47 Hour Firearms Training Course, 8-Hour Pre-Assignment, OJT, and Annual In-Service Training, individuals must provide the Department of State with either a copy of their Basic Course for Peace Officers certificate, or a letter from the academy indicating their academy training. These courses must meet or exceed the MPTC basis course without firearms. In addition, if the individual is in an armed position, the individual must have completed MPYC Basic Course for Peace Officer with Firearms, or both the Basic Course for Peace Officers without Firearms and Firearms and Deadly Physical Force [long firearms course]. If currently employed, the individual must also provide a copy of their ID card showing current employment, and that they are in good standing.

E. *NYS Corrections Officers as defined in NYS CPL, §2.10 (25):* (This does not include city or county correction officers.) In order to be exempt from the 47 Hour Firearms Training Course, 8-Hour Pre-Assignment, OJT, and

Annual In-Service Training, individuals must provide the Department of State with a letter from the NYS Department of Correctional Services and a copy of their ID card showing that they are currently employed as a NYS Corrections officer in good standing.

**Note:** Individuals who are no longer active peace officers and do not have a valid basic course certificate, or do not qualify for either a waiver or an exemption, must complete the 47 Hour Firearms Training Course, 8 Hour Pre-Assignment, and OJT.

# Index

Page numbers in italics refer to figures.